The world is full of complainers.

And the fact is, nothing comes with a guarantee. Now I don't care if you're the Pope of Rome, President of the United States or Man of the Year; something can all go wrong.

Now go on ahead, you know, complain, tell your problems to your neighbor, ask for help and watch him fly. Now, in Russia, they got it mapped out so that everyone pulls for everyone else – that's the theory, anyway. But what I know about is Texas, and down here you're on your own.

Visser, Blood Simple

By Jason Morningstar

Edited by Steve Segedy

Layout by Patrick Murphy and Jason Morningstar

Additional layout by Giulia Barbano

Color art and Cover by John Harper, *www.onesevendesign.com*

Additional art by Jason Morningstar

BOILERPLATE

This document uses the Hitchcock, Vertigo, and Meridien typefaces. *Fiasco* die font by the Madirishman.

Fiasco is copyright 2009 by Jason Morningstar. Color plates are copyright 2009 by John Harper. All rights are reserved.

If you'd like to create *Fiasco*-related content, we'd like to help. Write us at *info@bullypulpitgames.com*.

ISBN number 978-1-934859-39-1

Eleventh printing, October 2017

DEDICATION

To Autumn Winters, who loves a good fiasco.

THANKS

...to Jarrod Acquistapace, Ariele Agostini, Kevin Allen Jr, Giulia Barbano, Rob Bohl, Jason D. Corley, Adam Dray, Lara Ermacora, Damian Fraustro, Nathan Herrold, Will Hindmarch, William Huggins, Sage LaTorra, Flavio Mortarino, Renato Ramonda, Kira Scott, Jonathan Walton, Kamil Wegrzynowicz and my friends at story-games.com and elsewhere for insightful comments and enthusiasm.

Big thanks to Seth Ben-Ezra, Chris Bennett, Colin Creitz, Robert Earley-Clark, Lara Ermacora, Alessandro Fontana, Zach Greenvoss, Tom Gurganus, John Harper, Jeff Hosmer, Ralph Mazza, Robert Poppe, Graham Walmsley and Chris Yates for taking the time to help me make this game good as hell.

Heartfelt thanks to all of you, and to every playtester, too – and sorry about the mess out back under the tarp. Best not to look, OK? *I've got it all under control.*

PLAYTESTERS

Team Bull City: Mark Causey, Joel Coldren, Jonathan Davis, Matthew Gandy, Mike Graves, Nathan Herrold, Andy Kitkowski, Scott Morningstar, Clinton R. Nixon, Ian Oakes, Robert Poppe, Eric Provost, Lisa Provost, Dan "Buttercup" Puckett, Steve Segedy, Joe "Uncle Timothy" Stanton and Remi Treuer.

Team Do Not Use Our Real Names: Tomg, Spuds, Darth and Heli.

Team EndGame: Chris "That's my leopard" Bennett, Robert Earley-Clark, Chris Peterson, and Karen Twelves.

Team London: Steve Dempsey, Wai Kien, Simon Rogers, Graham Walmsley and Graham's friend Dave.

Team High Point: Chad Bowser, James "Connie" Jeffers, Andi "Chicken Hut" Newton, Chris Norwood, and Clarence Simpson.

Team Milan: Claudio Agosti, Silvia Bindelli, Claudio Criscione, Damiano Desco, and Flavio Mortarino.

Team Los Angeles: Eric J. Boyd, Josh Roby, Ryan Macklin and William Huggins.

Team Morristown: Lowell Carson, Eric Tage Larsen, Ryan Macklin and Michael "Preacher McKean" O'Sullivan.

Team Peoria: Crystal Ben-Ezra, Gabrielle Ben-Ezra, Seth Ben-Ezra, Ralph Mazza and Keith Sears.

Team Portland: Evan E. Dumas, Zach Greenvoss, Joe Jaquette, and Brian K. Smith.

Team Seattle: James Brown, Chris Bennett, Michael Decuir, Ryan Forsythe, Matthew "Tire King" Gagan, Will Huggins, Matthew Klein, Ching-Ping Lin, Ralph Mazza, Lesley McKeever, Lukas Myhan, Paul Riddle and Mike "Lucille" Sugarbaker.

Team Shot the Sheriff: Colin Creitz, John Daniels, Chris Deibler, Sarah "Heidi Jo" Thomas.

Team SuperNoVa: Jeff Hosmer, Auntie M, Joe Iglesias, Sean Leventhal, and Mel White.

TABLE OF CONTENTS

Front Matter 4

    Table of Contents 7

    Elevator Pitch 8

    Getting to the Good Stuff.. 9

    Overview 10

    Glossary 12

The Setup 15

Scenes.. 27

Act One.. 35

The Tilt 39

Act Two 43

The Aftermath 47

Optional Craziness 51

Tables 55

    Tilt Table 56

    Aftermath Table.. 58

Playsets 60

    Main Street 61

    Boomtown 71

    Suburbia 81

    The Ice... 91

Replay 101

Designer's Notes.. 122

Filmography 124

Cheat Sheet... 126

Resources 128

Index 129

THE ELEVATOR PITCH

Here are just a few of the key ingredients: Dynamite, pole vaulting, laughing gas, choppers – can you see how incredible this is going to be? Hang gliding, come on!

Dignan, Bottle Rocket

Fiasco is inspired by cinematic tales of small-time capers gone disastrously wrong – particularly films like *Blood Simple*, *Fargo*, *The Way of the Gun*, *Burn After Reading*, and *A Simple Plan*. You'll play ordinary people with powerful ambition and poor impulse control. There will be big dreams and flawed execution. It won't go well for them, to put it mildly, and in the end it will probably collapse into a glorious heap of jealousy, murder, and recrimination. Lives and reputations will be lost, painful wisdom will be gained, and if you are really lucky, your guy just might end up back where he started.

YOU'LL NEED

* Three, four, or five people, including yourself. There is no Game Master.

* Four six-sided dice per player, two each of black and white. You really just need two different colors you can use to denote success and failure – I'll use black and white for clarity.

* Several dozen index cards or sticky notes and some pencils.

* About two and a half hours, varying with experience, play style and the size of your group.

GETTING TO THE GOOD STUFF

There's a fly in the ointment, shit's hittin' the fan, the lion will speak!

Saul, Pineapple Express

JUST BROWSING

If you are browsing and want to get a feel for the game's flavor, read the Elevator Pitch on page 8, the Overview on page 10, and maybe the Glossary. Then check out the Playsets beginning on page 60 and the replay – an extended example of play – beginning on page 101.

NEW TO WEIRD GAMES

If this sort of game is new to you, I'd encourage you to read the whole thing and pay particular attention to the examples cross-referenced in the replay that starts on page 101. It isn't rocket science, and I hope it's pretty clear how it works, but it might be a little weird on first reading. The examples should help!

STORY GAMING GOOBER

If you are comfortable with collaborative, narrative-heavy games (*Fiasco* is similar in a lot of ways to *Prime Time Adventures* or *Montsegur 1244*, for example), you can get away with ignoring the Replay and the "Things to Look For" sections of the rules. It does behave a little differently than what you are used to, though, so don't make any assumptions. I try to spell out exactly what to do and when to do it.

FIASCO REGULAR

The cheat sheet is on page 126, the Tilt table is on page 56 and the Aftermath table is on page 58. Playsets begin on page 60. Go crazy.

OVERVIEW

Before we go any further, all right, we have to swear to God, Allah, that nobody knows about this but us, all right? No family members, no girlfriends, nobody.

Peter Gibbons, Office Space

Fiasco is a highly collaborative game in which every player should always be engaged – either actively playing a character or throwing out suggestions, brainstorming scene ideas, and listening for ways to make each scene hit harder than the last. Because the pace is so frantic, every choice you make has to matter a lot.

A game of *Fiasco* begins with **The Setup** – a group activity where you and your friends create a potent and unstable set of circumstances. You choose a Playset, which fixes the game in a particular time and place – a contemporary southern town, maybe, or the old west. Using a pile of dice, you create an interconnected circle of **Relationships** and **Details** pulled from the Playset. Once you've created a situation poised on the brink of juicy disaster, you define characters based on your choices.

Once the Setup is done, you play out **scenes**, which focus on various characters in rotation. When it is your turn, you get to choose whether you want to **Establish** the scene (setting the nature of the scene, any obvious conflict, the location, and the characters on hand) or **Resolve** it (leaving the initial set-up to your friends, but deciding on whether the outcome is positive or negative for your guy). You can't do both!

Play is divided into two acts. As a rule of thumb, each act ought to take about an hour. At the end of **Act One** is **the Tilt**, where some interesting and crazy things show up to disrupt the story. At the end of **Act Two** is **the Aftermath**, where you learn the ultimate fate of all your characters. Usually the Setup takes fifteen minutes, and the Tilt and Aftermath take another fifteen minutes total. Your playing time will vary a bit.

You'll have a bunch of dice (four per player), and these are used throughout the game in different ways. The dice aid in The Setup, help determine scene outcomes, and pace the game – when half of them have been used, Act One ends, The Tilt is determined, and Act Two begins. When all of the dice have been used, Act Two is over and it's time for the Aftermath.

In Act One you meet your characters, learn what they are after, and take some first steps toward getting them what they want. When the first act ends (after half the dice have been used), you add The Tilt that further destabilizes the situation. Then Act Two begins.

In Act Two, you drive toward clear goals for your characters – maybe quiet success, maybe theatrical revenge, or maybe just a warm place to sleep. After the last die has been used, you learn your respective characters' fates and begin the Aftermath.

The Aftermath is played as a montage, and once again the dice offer you a chance to reveal your character's fate in a colorful, fast-paced and sometimes surprising conclusion.

ONE LAST FUCKING THING

I tried to write these rules in a conversational style that suits the subject matter and the films it references. You can expect some foul language and salacious depictions of reprehensible behavior, which will likely be par for the course in play as well. If that sort of thing bothers you, this is probably not a game you will enjoy.

GLOSSARY

Look. Personally I don't give a shit. I know Marty's a hard-on but you gotta do something. I don't know; give the money back, say you're sorry, or get the fuck out of here, or something ... it's very humiliating, preaching about this shit ... I'm not laughing at this, Ray Bob, so you know it's no fucking joke.

Meurice, Blood Simple

Act: A unit of play consisting of half the game. Act One is preceded by the Setup and followed by the Tilt. Act Two is preceded by the Tilt and followed by the Aftermath.

Aftermath: The Aftermath occurs after Act Two. Played out in montage, the Aftermath gives everyone a chance to share their character's glorious future. Outcomes are determined by rolling the dice you've accumulated throughout the game, totaling each color, and subtracting the lower total from the higher. Resulting big numbers are good (black seven, for example), while trending toward zero is very bad.

Category: On each Playset table there are six general Categories. For example, on the object table there might be a Weapon Category. Each Category, in turn, has six specific Elements. These are chosen during Setup.

Detail: A Detail can be an Object, a Need, or a Location. It is always attached to a Relationship. You define them during the Setup by general Category and specific Element (like "Object: Weapon: Klingon Sword", for example), and the game revolves around them. Things injected at the Tilt are also a special sort of Detail.

Dice: *Fiasco* uses six-sided dice in a couple of different ways. They are a pacing mechanism, and an initial stockpile of four per player will gradually be reduced by half (ending Act One and triggering the Tilt) and then to zero (ending Act Two and triggering the Aftermath). In individual scenes, players will either choose or receive a single die whose color signals positive or negative outcome. During the Tilt and Aftermath, each color is added together and the smaller total is subtracted from the higher. Having a high number in either white or black is desirable, and in fact might save your poor guy's life in the Aftermath. A matched set of black and white dice is the kiss of death, or at least the kiss of powerful hurt.

Element: On each Playset table there are six general Categories, and within each Category are six specific Elements. Within the Weapon Category on the Object list, for example, there might be "a K-frame revolver". These are chosen during Setup.

Establish: One of the two ways you can approach your guy's scene – by framing it up, deciding who is involved, what it is about and where it is going down. If you choose to Establish, your friends get to Resolve.

Playset: The heart of a good fiasco – a combination of setting, situation, sub-genre, and kick in the pants. A Playset consists of four lists – Relationships, Needs, Objects, and Locations. The last three are collectively known as Details, and they are attached to particular Relationships.

Relationship: The game's core – the reason two characters are connected. Your character will have different Relationships with the characters played by your friends on your right and left at the table.

Resolve: One of the two ways you can approach your guy's scene – by allowing your friends to Establish, you can enjoy being surprised by how they frame the scene. In exchange for giving up that control, you get to decide whether the outcome is positive or negative for your guy – to Resolve the scene.

Setup: The prep stage for a *Fiasco* session, in which you choose a Playset, establish Relationships, attach Details to them, create characters, and figure out exactly what is going on.

Tilt: The Tilt occurs when half the game's dice have been allocated, which means when half the scenes have been played, immediately after Act One. In a four player game, the Tilt happens after eight scenes. It's when you learn what will happen to destabilize an already chaotic situation. Something might catch on fire, or someone might be arrested, or something really unfortunate might be accidentally left in a bus terminal to be found by the FBI. Tilt Elements can come into play at any time during Act Two – usually right away!

THE SETUP

THE BASICS

Choose a Playset.

Roll a bunch of dice into a central pile.

Develop a web of Relationships and Details.

Create characters attached to those Relationships and Details.

Put all the dice back into a central pile.

HOW IT WORKS

I've been to prison once; I've been married – twice. I was once drafted by Lyndon Johnson and had to live in shit-ass Mexico for two and a half years for no reason. I've had my eye socket punched in, a kidney taken out and I got a bone-chip in my ankle that's never gonna heal. I've seen some pretty shitty situations in my life, but nothing has ever sucked more ass than this.

Willie, Bad Santa

＊ Choose a Playset.

The Playset is *Fiasco*'s core – from it you'll draw situation, characters, and inspiration. Think of Playsets like trouble construction kits – you've got big lists of cool stuff, and each will have a flavor unique to its time and place.

Playsets are divided into four lists. The lists reflect the things that will be central to your game – the stock elements. Relationships will be first and foremost, and they'll be spiced up by Details that color and intensify Relationships. A Detail is always attached to a Relationship, and can be an Object, a Need, or a Location.

The Playset lists, in turn, are broken down into six general Categories and six specific Elements within each Category. For example, in the Nice Southern Town Playset, general Category three of Locations is "Out by the Interstate", and within that list, number four is "The Quik-Pik gas station and convenience store".

Choose a Playset everyone is excited about, or make your own (four awesome ready-to-play Playsets start on page 60, and there's advice on making your own, too).

＊ Roll a bunch of dice into a central pile.

Once you've chosen a Playset, roll some dice in the middle of the table – four per player, two black and two white. Thus, you'll be rolling 12, 16, or 20 dice, for three, four or five players, and they will be evenly split between black and white. It doesn't matter who rolls – just make sure you start the Setup with a nice random assortment of numbers.

★ Develop a web of Relationships and Details.

You've now chosen a Playset stuffed with interesting things, and have a pile of randomly-rolled dice. The next step is to combine the two.

Your particular game is going to have a bunch of specific bits associated with it, like "Location: The Suds and Duds Laundromat on Commerce Street" or "Relationship: Friends with benefits". Together these will form the bones of your game. The guy you make will have a pair of Relationships with other people in the community, played by your friends to your right and left, and a Detail – a Need, Object, or Location – to help fill out his particular background.

Start with the player who grew up in the smallest town and then take turns, building the web of information in rotation. You do this by looking over the Playset lists and grabbing a die from the central pile with a number that matches an Element you are interested in. If it's for a general Category (Like "Location: Out by the Interstate"), write it on a new index card. If it is filling in a specific Element for a general Category already on the table (like "Location: Out by the Interstate: The Quik-Pik"), add that to the card to finish it. Leave a die you allocate on top of its card, just to keep everything organized. Since there will be one Relationship between each pair of players, you can simplify The Setup by starting with two index cards per player, and writing "Relationship" at the top of one of them).

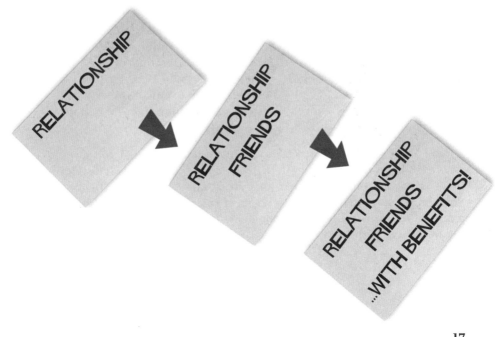

Details are always explicitly tied with Relationships – if there's a mink farm, it's a mink farm connected to the preacher and his secretary or the two cops on the take, not an individual character. It's perfectly acceptable to lay down a Relationship between two other players if it's still undefined. It's also totally OK to add a Detail to one of your own Relationships.

As you rotate around taking turns adding information, eventually you'll have two index cards per player, and every index card will have two dice on top of it – one for its general Category, and one for its specific Element. The only rules are:

* **One Relationship between each pair of neighboring players at the table.**

* **One Detail attached to each Relationship.**

* **At least one Need, one Location, and one Object.**

* **The last remaining die is wild, and can be any number.**

The first rule ensures you have a circle of interrelated characters. The second rule ensures that everybody has a connection to something cool and colorful (chances are you'll do this anyway). The third rule ensures that you have something to motivate misbehavior, and interesting things to misbehave with and around. The last rule ensures that the final die is actually fun to use.

You'll have precisely one Relationship between each pair of neighboring players (so one with the friend on your right and one with your friend on the left), and one Detail latched onto each Relationship. You must have at least one Object, Need, and Location. In a four or five player game, you'll have more Details – I suggest a second Need for four players, and then a second Location or Object for five. Once you've played a few times, feel free to ignore this advice. A five-player game with three Needs could be pretty fun.

As you build up the web of Relationships, talk about what you see and where it's heading. If you begin to flesh out the situation as it develops, that's fantastic – but don't think too hard about characters at this point. You should start to get a strong sense of inter-connectedness and see points of friction and potential mayhem. The Setup is pretty entertaining in its own right!

Once all the bits are in place, you should have a clear fiasco in the making. Somebody wants something they don't have, at a minimum. That's a good place to start. For more information about Needs, Objects, and Locations, and why they are cool, see pages 23–25. For an example of this in play, see page 102.

> *** Create characters attached to those Relationships and Details.**

At this point you have a big pile of intermingled Relationships, a dangerous obsession or two and some tasty places and things to wrap them around. At some point you might cry out "of course! I'm the librarian who is selling dope to the Board of Aldermen!", but it's also possible that your character remains amorphous. Now is the time to get it into focus, because leaving things to be fleshed out in play weakens them. Work as a team – everybody needs to define who they are, based on their particular pair of Relationships, and quite often these will be unequal, freighted by differences in power and status. It may make more sense for you to be the drug dealer, rather than the guy who also has to be the preacher – but maybe not!

Once you've firmed up the situation and everyone agrees it is solid, you are ready to play! You should have a pair of Relationships shared with the players on your right and left, some interesting Details associated with some of the Relationships, and a character that has emerged from the web of information you've generated as a group.

Give your character a name! It's helpful to write this on an index card, folded like a tent in front of you for everyone to see. Feel free to use the Relationship cards to add notes, names, and other information you want to keep track of.

> *** Put all the dice back into a central pile.**

This is the last thing you do before starting Act One. Clear off those cards and dump all the dice back into the center – number, facing and order don't matter. You'll be grabbing dice throughout the game, so keep them within easy reach.

THINGS TO LOOK FOR

A burglar broke in intending to loot the place, uh, repented, became despondent over his lifestyle and shot himself.

Freddy Bender, Intolerable Cruelty

CHARACTERS

As you engineer the fiasco, talk about what sort of people your characters might be, why they are in the Relationships they find themselves in, why the Details are important, and what's going on. Just don't pre-play the game or get fixated on a particular character too early. You don't have complete control over who your character ends up being, and you'll be defining him based on Relationships and Details that won't be fully fleshed out until near the end of the Setup. So don't think too hard about who your guy is just yet – concentrate on choosing interesting and perhaps challenging Elements as you put the fiasco together. Once all the glorious pieces are in place, then you'll have a chance to build up a great character. So cool it at first and see what happens.

Here's an important point – your guy may not be in trouble. The game's central dilemma may not be about your character at all – maybe he's a distant relative, or a do-gooder, or just collateral damage. If it turns out your guy isn't in a jam as the game begins, focus on making the jam more intense until it touches him, too. Trust me, eventually it will.

Some Relationships are balanced and others are not. Some are very specific and some are amorphous. You may find yourself with a pair of oddly competing Relationships – this is strictly awesome! Feel free to interpret loosely if that helps. Many Relationships imply a power differential – con man and mark, for example – and it may be helpful to work out who is who based on the two characters' other Relationships.

20

SITUATION

As you gradually build the game elements up, bits of situation will start to emerge – encourage this and go with it. You have unlimited freedom in interpreting the meaning and positioning of the Elements that are brought into the game. At a minimum you'll need to sort out who is who if the Relationship is unequal, and some adjustment will probably be necessary to make all the Relationships mesh well. For example, if one character is the mayor, and he has a Relationship with his son-in-law, it makes sense for the son-in-law to in turn be in a Relationship with the mayor's daughter – his wife. That said, just because two characters are co-workers doesn't mean you can't just decide they are also husband and wife as well – and the Chicken Hut can also be a meth lab. Adding Details will change things in surprising and cool ways – again, The Setup is a collaborative process so have fun and be flexible. When in doubt, make characters related!

Sometimes it might take some creative monkey-wrenching – in one game I had a guy who had a Relationship and Location that clearly demanded he be a high school student, but his other Relationship was "corrupt official and local big shot". My teenager might make a very strange corrupt official, but in a small town the captain of the football team is definitely a local big shot...

RELATIONSHIPS AND DETAILS

True fiascos revolve around Details, which are expressly tied to Relationships – for example, (stay with me here; I'm sketching out an entire session) Val and I have characters with a Relationship as co-workers, and we share a Location – the Quik-Pik. My Quik-Pik manager and Glenn's drunken kid have a Relationship as father and son, and we share an Object – a vintage car. Glenn's drunk and Val's Quik-Pik employee have a Relationship – lovers – and they share a Need – to get even with a rival. It'll be our job to stitch the Details and Relationships into a fun and messed-up situation. Don't make the mistake of locking a Detail very tightly to a single character – lock it to the Relationship instead!

See how that works? With a little imagination the example above becomes pretty interesting. I've got a hard-working dad who has rebuilt a muscle car with his son to keep him off the sauce, and the kid and his girlfriend (who works for me and steals booze right under my nose) are using it to try to beat her ex-boyfriend in illegal street races for pink slips – a pink slip Glenn's character doesn't have. So everything is cool as long as he keeps winning...

PLAYER
THREE

LOCATION
MACTOWN
THE CARP SHOP
TOOL SHED

OBJECT
FORBIDDEN
HIDDEN HYDROPONICS

RELATIONSHIP
CRIME
DRUG PEOPLE

RELATIONSHIP
SOUL
LIFERS ON
THE ICE

PLAYER
TWO

RELATIONSHIP

WORK

SPECIALIST/
SUPPORTER

NEED

TO GET EVEN

WITH A SCIENTIST

PLAYER
ONE

NEEDS

All I ever wanted was to measure up to my father.

Ed, *L.A. Confidential*

Needs stem from unmet desire. Somebody wants something (or someone) they do not have. The "wanter" might be one member of the Relationship, it might be both, or it might be a third person they both deeply care about. Regardless, both members of the Relationship stand to benefit or suffer equally. For a Need to really kick, both characters need to be heavily invested in it – possibly at cross purposes, but always invested. Obsessed, even! Is your guy's Need to get respect from a family member by rescuing them from ruin? It's perfectly acceptable for one half of the Relationship to be the family member in need of rescue. It'd also be fine to make the person on the brink of ruin external to the Relationship – maybe your two characters are parents out to save their child. The key is that if it all goes wrong, they both get dragged down.

Somebody needs to Need something problematic to have a genuine fiasco, but it's important to note that not every Relationship needs a Need – in fact, the game is more fun if Needs are a little thin on the ground. Let some characters start the game removed from destructive motivation – maybe they will be a force for reason and good throughout the game, or maybe they will be caught up in the spiral of failure and destruction that will surely touch them at some point. Some questions to ask:

* Is the Need capable of being the obsessive core of the Relationship?

* Is the Need alive with possibility, both good and bad (but mostly bad)?

* Is the Need producing nods of appreciation and excitement from your friends?

If the answer to each is a resounding yes, you've got a fun Need.

LOCATIONS

Well, here we are in a room with two manky hookers and a racist dwarf.

Ken, In Bruges

Locations should be metaphoric extensions of characters. These are places that serve as windows to the souls of the people associated with them, and you should return to them again and again. You can shape both the character and the place in partnership with the player you share a Relationship with. Does a married banker keep his mistress-secretary in a split-level duplex? That's more than a building, that's a way of life, and says a lot about their relationship. During the game, if you're looking for a place to have a scene happen, scan around for existing Locations. If somebody cared enough to author the Chicken Hut out by the interstate, it ought to be a hub of in-game activity. Where else are you going to find an industrial fryer? Some questions to ask:

* Is the Location capable of being absolutely central to the Relationship?

* Is the Location able to backdrop lots of characters in different ways?

* Is the Location sparking ideas for scenes before it hits the table?

If the answer to each is an enthusiastic yes, you've got a great Location.

OBJECTS

Fifteen million dollars is not money. It's a motive with a universal adapter on it.

Joe Sarno, The Way of the Gun

Objects also make statements about characters and will help drive play. Think of them as physical stand-ins for the Relationship to which they are tied. Do the frowsy laundromat attendant and her live-in boyfriend share some legal records? Maybe they are adoption papers, or maybe they are a bequest. Either way, those papers are going to show up in the first part and – count on it – probably result in somebody's death by the end of the story. Don't be afraid to introduce an Object tied to another Relationship into your scenes, further entangling your character in their lives. Some questions to ask:

* Is the Object capable of being equally important to both sides of the Relationship?

* Is the Object a clear magnet for trouble of various types?

* Is the Object clearly going to have a life of its own, rather than being useless color?

If the answer to each is a fist-pumping yes, you've got a perfect Object.

SOME FINAL THOUGHTS ON DETAILS

Bind Details together, and come back to them again and again. Once they've been defined one or the other should crop up in pretty much every scene. However innocuous a Detail seems, it should be a fountain of trouble – and often, the most mundane Details are the strongest choices. In one game we had a property deed – pretty boring stuff as Objects go, right? Turns out the whole game hinged on that deed, and two people died over it. Every character was connected in some way to it – a father and daughter both wanted it for their own reasons, a hapless ex-husband had it fair and square, and the deed was to the house the cute southern girl in love with the ex-husband rented.

On a related note, sometimes a Detail won't gain much of a narrative foothold. That's OK, let it go. As long as the game's kicking, one weak Detail won't hurt anything. In the same game with the property deed, the father and the cute southern girl shared a Need that was largely ignored from start to finish. No big deal, ultimately. That said, if tweaking a Detail a tiny bit will make it fit the game and come alive, don't be shy – tweak away. If "To get the truth about what she did..." really ought to be "To get the truth about what he did..." well, just change it already.

YOU'RE GOOD TO GO

The Setup is over at this point – Act One awaits. Once you've finished The Setup, actual play is structured in two acts. These consist of scenes, which are the meat and potatoes of the game, so we'll discuss how those work first before moving on to the over-arching structure. You'll use the rules for scenes during the majority of the game.

SCENES

Scenes exist so we can ask and answer questions – sometimes directly, sometimes not. Each and every one should result in something cool and interesting happening. Your character's stories will move forward based on the strange and tragic outcomes of your scenes.

THE BASICS

When it is your turn, your character is in the spotlight. Choose to Establish or Resolve the scene.

If you are Establishing, create a scene. If you are Resolving, ask your friends to create a scene for your character.

Begin the scene. At some point during the scene, determine the outcome.

If you Established, your friends will give you a white or black die signaling a positive or negative outcome for your character. If you chose to Resolve, you pick the die and the outcome.

If it is Act One, hand the die you are given back to another player. If it is Act Two, keep the die you choose.

Finish the scene, informed by the color choice.

HOW IT WORKS

Look honey, I'm going to be working some strange hours over the next week or two, so don't ask me what I'm doing because I don't want to lie to you.

Terry Leather, The Bank Job

* **When it is your scene, your character is in the spotlight. Choose to Establish or Resolve.**

When your turn rolls around, your first choice is which part of the scene you want to have control over – how it begins, or how it ends. You can Establish a scene or Resolve it, but not both!

YOU ESTABLISH   THEY RESOLVE

* **If you are Establishing, create a scene.**

If you choose to Establish the scene, you have the privilege of acting as director. Who is present? Do any Objects or Locations factor into it? Does it address a Need? When does it take place – is it a flashback, concurrent with other scenes we've already played, or at some other time? Establishing scenes is the most common and direct approach. Maybe you absolutely, positively, want to confront the Mexican gangster who is terrorizing your boyfriend. Awesome! Put your guy in the middle of the action, frame the scene, and play it out. Look at the cards on the table, consider the emerging story, and pull some elements together. Tap people to play side characters as needed, but be as economical as you can with stuff that wasn't authored during the Setup – always use what you have unless you absolutely need to bring in something else. For an example of Establishing a scene with an obvious conflict, see page 109.

THEY ESTABLISH   YOU RESOLVE

* If you are Resolving, ask your friends to create a scene for your character.

Your other option is to Resolve the scene. Maybe you want more control over your guy's destiny. Maybe you are just out of ideas! Choosing to Resolve the scene means that you are putting the director's responsibilities in the hands of your friends. It's their job to make the scene about something you, as a player, want – or maybe don't want. Rest assured they will surprise, delight, and horrify you. You can make suggestions, but the composition of the scene – who, what, where – is out of your hands. Asking to Resolve is a signal that you also want an obvious conflict. For an example of choosing to Resolve a scene, see page 114.

* Begin the scene. At some point during the scene, determine the outcome.

At a minimum you'll have the outline of a scene – where it takes place, who is there, and what they are doing. You might also have a big conflict in mind, but it's perfectly acceptable to find out what's going on in play as well. You can Establish a scene and see where it leads, if that feels right to you. Of course if you chose to Resolve, your friends will set the scene and probably introduce a conflict for you.

There aren't any hard and fast rules about what constitutes a good scene or what constitutes an acceptable level of "positive outcome" or its opposite. Ideally you want all your friends involved and throwing in ideas, an opportunity for some character interaction, incorporation of stuff you've authored into the game, and questions both asked and answered. Your group will have its own standards and style – just avoid scenes that are aimless, don't advance the plot in an interesting way, or are self indulgent. You don't get very many scenes! Make them count. Be bold.

* If you Established, accept a die from your friends. If you Resolved, choose a die and the outcome.

If you are Resolving, at any time during the scene you can take any die that remains in the central pile, white or black. If you take a white die, that is a signal that the outcome of the scene will be positive for your character. If you take a black die, it's the opposite – a negative outcome for your character.

If you Established the scene, your friends will make this decision for you, reaching a decision about which die to give you however they like. Whether you decide the outcome based on character- or player-level choices is up to you.

No matter who chooses the die, hold it up for everyone to see and then carry on – you don't need to disrupt the scene at all. The color of the die you've chosen will let everyone know how the scene is supposed to play out. Once you know whether the end result is going to be good or bad for your guy, you can play out the rest of the scene. I can't emphasize enough how satisfying it is to do all this without skipping a beat in the role-playing – just play the scene, accept the die, and let that guide everyone to an appropriate conclusion. That said, it's also perfectly acceptable to interrupt a scene to announce your intent, to point out something that's worth fighting about, or to ask for clarification.

Many times you'll frame a scene as a straight-ahead conflict. Do you convince the Sheriff to arrest your sister? If throwing your sister in jail is a net positive for your character, a white die means she's in bracelets. Scenes don't need to be centered on conflicts, though. Sometimes really good scenes are just color, giving us insight into a character's heart and mind. Positive and negative can be a little more subtle here. Ultimately if it is your scene, you decide what constitutes a positive outcome or a negative one. Sometimes you'll need to communicate this if it isn't entirely clear, and that's encouraged. It's also possible a scene won't involve any role-playing at all – just description. If that's what's called for, there's no need to shoe-horn role-playing into the scene.

★ If it is Act One, give the outcome die to another player. If it is Act Two, keep the outcome die.

As the game progresses you'll develop a little pile of dice. Keep them in the open in front of you – you'll need them later. Note that the point values of the dice don't matter right now – just the colors. During the Tilt and the Aftermath, having a collection of dice well balanced between black and white will spell disaster, and having lots of one color and few or none of the other is a recipe for safety and success.

In Act One, you always give away the outcome die if it is your scene. Give it to any other player you like. This decision has nothing to do with the in-game fiction and everything to do with who you want to support or mess with.

In Act Two, you always keep the outcome die if it is your scene. This means choosing to Resolve is especially inviting, just when losing control over scene framing becomes a terrible idea.

★ Finish the scene, informed by the color choice.

If you end up with a white die, the outcome should be positive for your guy. If you end up with a black die, the outcome should be negative. How positive or negative? That's up to you and your friends, guided by the tone you've set for the game in general and the scene in particular.

You'll have some unfinished business, and maybe a chance for some good role-playing, once the outcome is revealed. Enjoy it! That's how scenes work. Acts One and Two are nothing but scenes, in rotation, one after the other.

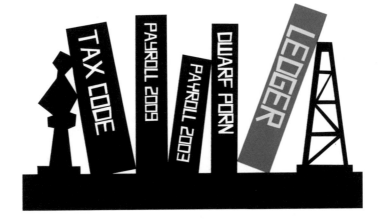

THINGS TO LOOK FOR

I wish somebody else had found that money.

Jacob Mitchell, A Simple Plan

THE FIRST SCENE

Sometimes *Fiasco*'s "cold start" beginning can be daunting. You've got a situation that seems primed for fun, but how do those translate into action? The answer is to take a look at the character in the spotlight and start asking questions.

Always build a scene for the guy in the spotlight around a question you'd love to see answered. What does he want to know about other characters, the world, himself? Do you wonder what would happen if he shorted his dealer? Does he wonder if lying to a cop is a good idea – or if lying *on top* of a cop is a good idea? Do you wonder if he has the balls to stand up to his dad? Sure, he got Shontelle pregnant and now his baby daughter is an Object in play (charming), but what does she know that keeps a maggot like him from running out on her?

Don't be shy. You have few enough opportunities to create scenes, so go big when you get the chance.

SOME ADVICE FOR KNUCKLEHEADS

The way scenes are Established and Resolved in *Fiasco* might seem a little counter-intuitive. To be perfectly clear, you don't set stakes as such (although it's OK to say what you want), you don't roll the die to determine an outcome, and the only limits on your description are those imposed by your friends on a social level – if they balk, figure it out together as players, with you (the player whose character is in the spotlight) having the final say. It's up to you to incorporate positive and negative outcomes into the developing story with their help and input. With a little practice this can be very smooth, but when in doubt, let the guy in the spotlight decide.

If you're Resolving, just grab a die mid-scene when you've decided how it's going to go. Make sure everybody sees it and continue the scene without missing a beat. Similarly, if you and your friends are making the call, somebody with a strong feeling can pick up a die and seek consensus exclusively through eye contact. It's pretty fun to handle this stuff without breaking stride.

Regardless of whether your friend chooses to Establish or Resolve his scene, you are involved. It's up to everybody at the table to either craft a memorable, engaging scene (if he asked to Resolve) or collectively determine the tenor of the outcome (if he chose to Establish). Either way, work together and do the most interesting thing you can. If you can't agree on a course of action, ask the player whose scene it is for help, and let him be the final arbiter of any log jam. Honestly, if you can't agree on this stuff it probably speaks to a bigger problem, and it might be worth taking a break to talk about it.

One last piece of advice – edit aggressively. Cut to the meat of a scene, don't beat around the bush, and wrap it up when a decision has been made, a truth has been discovered, or a Rubicon has been crossed.

WHY DIE CHOICE MATTERS

Here's the thing – the dice are both a countdown clock and a barometer of happiness and misery. There will be a bunch of dice in the central pile at the beginning of the game and none at the end. There are a finite number of positive and negative scenes, as defined by white and black dice, and players with lots of one or the other will get to make more interesting choices.

That said, it's generally a good idea to angle toward white or black, either by having negative outcomes and failing a lot, or by enjoying success and positive outcomes. During the Tilt and again during the Aftermath players will be rolling their own dice, totaling each color, and subtracting the high total from the low. Big numbers are good, low numbers, or zero, are bad.

As a result, there is a tactical element to all of this that can be really fun. While you can create a scene about anything, you're wasting everybody's time unless the results really matter to you. Figure out what you want – in the fiction or dice – and Establish a scene where you can make getting it interesting and attractive to your friends. If you want that white die in Act Two, you need to Establish a scene where they will absolutely want you to succeed – because if you let *them* Establish, they will surely make you want to fail! Likewise, if you are asked to create a scene for somebody to Resolve, think about what they might want and give them an impossible choice to make. In Act One the die they choose will be given away – possibly to you – so make sure the outcome really matters.

IT'S NOT ALL ABOUT YOU, TRUST ME

The game's action might drift toward the people with written Needs, but it isn't their story, necessarily. See the movie Fargo for a great example of a story that isn't really about the jackasses in the center of the storm, and see this game's extended example of play for some good examples of Establishing scenes, on pages 112 and 115.

WHY COLOR SCENES ARE GREAT

Scenes that don't go for the throat – monologues, narrated montages, character-driven moments that are revelatory and cool – are great. Every group will set its own tone and style concerning what constitutes a good conflict-free scene, as well as what defines positive and negative regarding the die awarded for the scene. One hard and fast rule, though – you always Establish your own. If you ask to Resolve, your friends should feel obligated to throw you a meaty conflict to chew on. Anything less would be weak sauce.

HEY, YOU JUST KILLED ME

In any session of *Fiasco* there is a good chance that people are going to perish. Your character is not immune from the carnage and may die. If this happens, it isn't a big deal – Character death just means that your scenes will either be flashbacks or won't include direct conflicts, you being dead and all. Your scenes should still be all about what your character wanted, and you can absolutely include other characters. It might be fun to use flashbacks to zero in on why he did what he did, using his untimely demise as a starting – rather than ending – point. The Aftermath should be about your character's goals, ambitions, or reputation rather than their physical person. Playing a dead character is liberating and expands your possibilities in interesting ways, while limiting you in others.

It's probably polite not to murder any characters before Act Two, and a person with a dead character is a good candidate for playing the various secondary ne'er-do-wells who tend to crop up during the game as well.

ACT ONE

In the first act, we should meet our guys and see the dynamics of their Relationships in action. Everything you do should foreshadow things to come. If we meet an overbearing father, he's going to get a hell of a lot more overbearing later – and rebelled against. If we see a machete, it's going to hack some stuff to pieces later in the game. Use this time to set things up and begin to knock them down.

THE BASICS

Take turns. When it is your turn, your character gets a scene.

When only half the dice remain in the central pile, Act One ends.

HOW IT WORKS

A few clues for latecomers: Several weeks ago... A pile of money... An English class... A house by the river... A romantic young girl...

Le Narrateur, Bande à Part

ACT ONE

★ **Take turns. When it is your turn, your character gets a scene.**

The player who grew up in the smallest town has the first scene. Rotate clockwise thereafter. See the rules for crafting scenes, which start on page 27. For an example of starting Act One, see the replay on page 108.

IN ACT ONE, GIVE THE OUTCOME DIE AWAY!

★ **When only half the dice remain in the central pile, Act One ends.**

When everybody has had two scenes, the game is just about half over. If you've got a solid Setup and have pushed hard, by this point you'll have a hell of a mess well underway.

THINGS TO LOOK FOR

There's no money, there's no weed. It's all been replaced by a pile of corpses.

Tom, Lock Stock and Two Smoking Barrels

BUILDING ACROSS ACT ONE

By the end of Act One, people should be aggressively pursuing their goals and maybe even achieving them. People with Needs ought to be chasing them hard, or starting to satisfy them. Encourage both poignant and revelatory color scenes and down and dirty, hilarious conflicts.

Keep an eye on those dice! It's easy to forget to end Act One at the half-way point. If your group has a problem with this, randomly parcel out the dice into two piles of equal number and only touch one pile per Act.

PLAYING TOWARD THE ENDGAME

In the Aftermath, dice are rolled and totaled as in the Tilt, but color has new meaning. On the Aftermath table, black results are generally physical in nature, while white results are generally social, mental, or emotional. So having a low black total means getting beaten up or crippled, while a low white result is probably emotional trauma or a ruined reputation. More importantly, having a high black or white total in the Aftermath means a good outcome for your character. Having a low number or zero – because you have no dice or your totals canceled out – means a terrible outcome for your character.

So why does it matter what color of dice you accumulate during the game? If you want to be able to choose new Details during the Tilt, you'll want more of one color than the other, so that you'll get either a high black or white total. Likewise if you want a happy ending in the Aftermath you'll want a lot of one color or the other. So if you have a specific destiny in mind for your character, angle for the right dice accordingly.

See "Good Die, Bad Die" in the Optional Craziness section on page 53 for another way to handle the Aftermath.

When half the dice have been taken from the communal pile, Act One ends. The break between the acts is the time when something new and unstable is injected into the story. This is called...

THE TILT

THE BASICS

At the end of Act One, roll the dice in front of you. Do some dice math.

If you have the high number of either color, you will help add a pair of complications. Roll the unused dice in the central pile.

Consult the Tilt table on page 56 and choose two Elements.

Reassemble the central die pile. Keep dice already assigned in Act One.

Take a break; stretch and get a snack. Talk about where the game is heading.

HOW IT WORKS

Up is down, black is white.

Eddie Dane, Miller's Crossing

* At the end of Act One, roll the dice in front of you. Do some dice math.

As Act One wraps up, you'll have some dice in front of you as the result of the preceding scenes. Roll them all, and add all the black dice together and all the white dice together, and then subtract the lower from the higher. For example, if you have one black and one white die, and roll 6 and 4 respectively, that's 2 black. If you had one black and three white dice, and rolled totals of 1 and 18 respectively, that's 17 white. If you have no dice, your total is zero. For an example of calculating your Tilt score, see page 117.

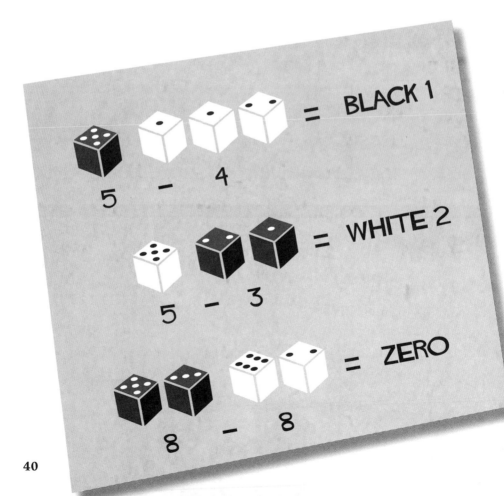

* If you have the highest number of either color, you will help add a pair of complications.

The player with the highest white total and the player with the highest black total each get to choose Tilt Elements. The Tilt is a standard list of Details, just like Needs, Objects, and Locations – but this time, it represents disruptive, game-changing events, people, and impulses.

* **Roll the unused dice in the central pile.**

You'll want some random numbers. In a four-person game, you'll have eight dice. Don't mix these with the dice you've earned in Act One.

* **Consult the Tilt table on page 56 and choose two Elements.**

Use the results of the roll to pick Elements from the Tilt list, as during the Setup. Each high-scoring player chooses a general Category and a specific Element for the *other* guy's Category. This is a good time to ask for input from the other players, who may have really good ideas. It's also a good time to privilege your own character's big finish!

Pick Tilt Elements you are excited about and will have the potential to take the game in an intriguing direction. You are injecting trouble, so don't be shy. Write the new Details on their own index cards and put them in the center of the table. These are fair game for anybody and are not Relationship-specific. Chances are everyone will know right where they belong. There's an example of creating Tilt Details in the replay, on page 118.

* **Reassemble the central die pile. Keep dice already assigned in Act One.**

Any dice used to choose Tilt Elements get tossed back into the central pile, which should be half empty. The other half of the game's dice should have already been assigned to players during Act One.

* **Take a break; stretch and get a snack. Talk about where the game is heading.**

Once you've got a pair of juicy Tilt Elements, discuss the events so far and what you'd like to see happen. Take a break and step away from the table, get a snack, and talk about the game. Check in with your friends, make sure everybody is having fun, and highlight cool things that have happened, and cool things that seem poised to happen. This break is actually really important!

THINGS TO LOOK FOR

He was alive when I buried him.

Ray, Blood Simple

DON'T BE A WUSS

Maybe you know exactly what you want for the Tilt, and there's a perfect thing just sitting there. Sometimes, though, it is way better to shake things up with something unexpected, incongruous, or downright mysterious. Just because you introduce "love rears its ugly head" doesn't mean you have to know how that is going to happen.

WEIRD EDGE CASES

If you end Act One without any dice, your total is a perfect zero for both black and white.

If you end Act One with only white dice or only black dice, that's a good thing – you're likely to have a high total one way or the other.

If the high black or high white score is a tie, have each tying player re-roll all of their dice. Highest total wins.

If no one has any dice of one color (that is, all the outcomes from Act One were positive or negative) the winners are the highest and lowest total of that color.

ACT TWO

Act Two is where the wheels should start to come off. Things are going wrong. New problems have emerged. Fires – metaphorical and maybe literal – will need to be fought. This is where you unscrew the jar of crazy and throw the lid at someone.

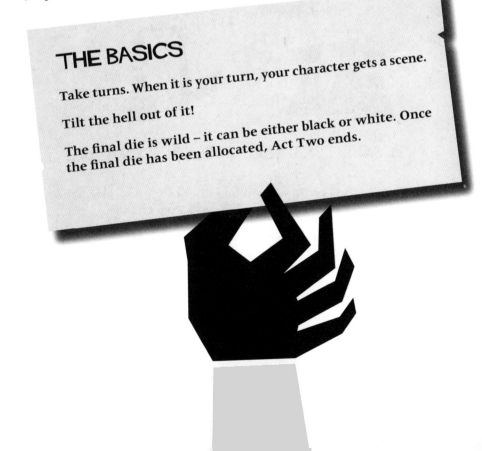

THE BASICS

Take turns. When it is your turn, your character gets a scene.

Tilt the hell out of it!

The final die is wild – it can be either black or white. Once the final die has been allocated, Act Two ends.

HOW IT WORKS

Tim, you're just a lost ball in the high weeds.

Reno Smith, Bad Day at Black Rock

* Take turns. When it is your turn, you get a scene.

Start Establishing or Resolving scenes again, just like you did in Act One. As before, you should keep dice in front of you as you receive them from yourself or others. You're adding to the dice you acquired in Act One. Eventually, after everybody has had two scenes, all the dice will be allocated and the central pile will be empty.

* Tilt the hell out of it!

Tilt Elements can make an appearance at any time during Act Two – right away, at the last minute, whenever it makes sense. But you should keep them in mind and drive toward them. If you know there's going to be some "confusion, followed by pain," set up a confusing situation and trust your friends to provide the pain.

IN ACT TWO, KEEP THE OUTCOME DIE!

* The final die is wild – it can be either black or white. Once the final die has been allocated, Act Two ends.

The last die of the game can be positive or negative, regardless of its color. Just like allowing the last die during The Setup to be any number, this takes away any sense of predestination – if you don't choose to Resolve the scene, your friends will probably stick you with exactly what you don't want. Of course, you can still get forced into a particular outcome in the *next* to last scene...

THINGS TO LOOK FOR

Well, I've flown seven million miles. And I've been waiting on people almost 20 years. The best job I could get after my bust was Cabo Air, which is the worst job you can get in this industry. I make about sixteen thousand, with retirement benefits that ain't worth a damn. And now with this arrest hanging over my head, I'm scared. If I lose my job I gotta start all over again, but I got nothing to start over with. I'll be stuck with whatever I can get. And that shit is scarier than Ordell.

Jackie Brown, Jackie Brown

DON'T FORGET THE LAST DIE IS WILD!

It can be either color. Make it a good one!

BUILDING ACROSS ACT TWO

When the last die has been claimed, Act Two ends. Build toward this – the dice are a pacing mechanism, so you've always got a good idea where you are in the story. Your goal should be to get your guy to a satisfactory conclusion – or near one – by the time the dice run out. Once they do, you've only got the Aftermath to finish your character's story, which will be fast and uncertain.

AS THEY LAY FOR THE AFTERMATH

That last die is wild – you can call it black or white, but use it as it lays for calculating the Aftermath. If it's actually white, just let it be white. It's much simpler than trying to calculate it as a special case if you used "last die wild" to make a white die black or vice-versa.

THE
AFTER

MATH

The Aftermath is usually the game's denouement. It's likely that the action has peaked, and that's totally OK. By this point we can probably see each character's general trajectory, but there's still time for tragic and unwholesome surprises. The Aftermath should be told in montage, and it should be fast.

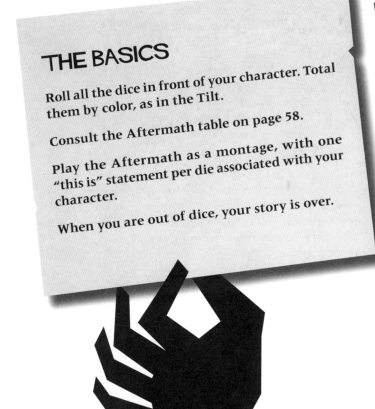

THE BASICS

Roll all the dice in front of your character. Total them by color, as in the Tilt.

Consult the Aftermath table on page 58.

Play the Aftermath as a montage, with one "this is" statement per die associated with your character.

When you are out of dice, your story is over.

HOW IT WORKS

So that was Mrs. Lundegaard on the floor in there. And I guess that was your accomplice in the wood chipper. And those three people in Brainerd. And for what? For a little bit of money. There's more to life than a little money, you know. Don'tcha know that? And here ya are, and it's a beautiful day. Well. I just don't understand it.

Marge Gunderson, Fargo

✶ Roll all the dice in front of your character. Total them by color, as in the Tilt.

At the end of Act Two, you'll have a modest pile of dice in front of you – including all the dice allocated to your character from both acts. Roll your dice, and again add all the black dice together and all the white dice together, and then subtract the lower from the higher. You should have about twice as many as before, because you keep the dice you were allocated during the first act!

Note that if you ended up with the game's final die, and it was decided that it was the opposite color, you can ignore that now. Other than choosing the outcome for the final scene, this choice has no effect – you don't have to remember that a white die is actually black when rolling the Aftermath.

✶ Consult the Aftermath table on page 58.

The Aftermath chart will give you your marching orders for the game's finale. Black results are generally physical and white results are generally social, mental, or emotional. You really, really don't want those dice to cancel each other out – the further from zero your final result, the happier the ending. At this point the game enters the final phase, the Aftermath. Check out the replay for an example on page 119.

* Play the Aftermath as a montage, with one "this is" statement per die associated with your character.

Here's the format – you take one of the dice that ended up in front of you and say "This is (my character), (doing something)." It should be active, and it should be about your guy, not somebody else. Then somebody else takes a die and does the same thing – you're describing the outcome of the game, maybe tightly focused, maybe meandering across many years. Your group will find its own preferred way of handling the montage. Keep it brisk, broad, colorful, and poignant.

* When you are out of dice, your story is over.

When the dice are gone, the game is over. If you end the game with few dice (it can happen!) not only will your poor guy have a horrible outcome but you've got precious little say in the matter. Maybe you just disappear. That said, chances are some character's Aftermaths will be more complicated than others, and tossing a die to a friend so they can have a satisfying ending isn't a crime. Similarly, if you have more dice than story, that's cool, too.

THINGS TO LOOK FOR

I'm not apologizing for what I did. I'm apologizing for what I didn't do.

Violet, Bound

WHATEVER YOU DO, KEEP IT SNAPPY

A typical Aftermath lasts five or ten minutes. If everybody's outcome is painfully obvious, maybe your game peaked really early and you only need to wrap things up. Forget the dice and montage and just craft epilogues in that case!

LIFE IS FULL OF SURPRISES

The results of the Aftermath table may surprise you, or even throw your character's story arc completely for a loop. Perhaps you'll roll exceptionally well and have a happy ending, even though the tail end of Act Two saw your guy handcuffed in the trunk of a Corolla that had been set on fire. These things happen – maybe the "happy ending" is more metaphor than reality, or maybe he made a daring and improbable escape that changes his life forever.

THIS IS SO UNFAIR

Is it weird that you can wallow in failure the entire game, collect a ton of black dice from all those bad scenes, and then have a happy ending? I'd point to the source material – in the films *Fiasco* references, true sad sacks often come out smelling like a rose. And the guy who never fails, who gets exactly what he wants – well, that guy's there so you can grind your teeth in impotent rage as he walks away scot-free. It's the people in the middle, with some ups and some downs, who really get screwed. Help your friends be in the middle.

OPTIONAL CRAZINESS

THE RULES TWEAKS

Sweating the Details

Hitting the Accelerator

Flirting With Disaster

Honoring the Last Die

Good Die, Bad Die

TWEAKING YOUR FIASCO

This may hurt.

Arthur Burns, The Proposition

These rules are entirely optional. Some of them address specific modes of play, and some of them are just fun variations. Add them to your *Fiasco* session at your own risk.

SWEATING THE DETAILS

Add or subtract dice to pace the game differently. As a rule of thumb, eight dice equals one hour of play. Going over 20 dice is counter-productive (as is trying to play with six people – play two three person games instead), but 14-16 dice is great for a three-player game and 18 is good for five players as well. It's also possible to build your situation and then discard some dice immediately for a shorter game. Obviously, add and subtract in pairs, and allow multiple Details to stack onto a single Relationship if necessary. Just make sure every character is associated with at least one Detail.

HITTING THE ACCELERATOR

If your game is moving very fast and is going to peak early, a protracted Act Two might be a bit of a grind. Instead of dragging things out, hit the gas and end early. Instead of two scenes per player in Act Two, just do one and make it count. Each should specifically include a Tilt Element and definitively resolve things for a particular character. You'll end the game with one loose die per player – since the Aftermath is built with these in mind, go ahead and have everybody assign a remaining die to another player in turn.

FLIRTING WITH DISASTER

You can stack the deck toward positive or negative outcomes. I suggest amping up the black die total a bit for a truly messed up cascade of miserable clusterfucks. This makes positive outcomes all the more precious, because they will be so painfully rare.

EXTRAS

HONORING THE LAST DIE

By default, the last die during The Setup and the last die of Act Two are wild – the color is defined by the player who picks it up. This makes them a little more interesting and a lot less pre-determined. Tossing this rule does no harm and has its own weird consequences – you might be put into a situation where you are forced to succeed, for example, or forced to make a mink farm central to your session. If that degree of determinism sounds fun, play the last die as it lies.

GOOD DIE, BAD DIE

Some groups will want to add a little extra morality to their Aftermath. You can do this by tweaking the endgame mechanic in a simple way – instead of each die being a "this is me" statement, require that the narration also be tied to the die color. White dice indicate generally positive or redemptive statements, and black dice indicate negative or harmful statements. Playing with this rule in effect will change die handling throughout the game in an interesting way.

TABLES

They snatched my narcotics and hightailed it outta there. Would've gotten away with it, but your son, fuck-head that he is, left his driver's license in a dead guy's hands.

Vincenzo Cocotti, True Romance

Unlike the tables built into Playsets, the Tilt and Aftermath tables are shared across Playsets – any game of *Fiasco* can rely on the same pair of tables. The Tilt destabilizes the action mid-game, and the Aftermath points toward character's individual outcomes at the end. Some Playsets may include a custom set of tables, in which case you should use those.

TILT TABLE

1 MAYHEM

⚀ An out of control rampage

⚁ A frantic chase

⚂ A dangerous animal (perhaps metaphorical) gets loose

⚃ Magnificent self-destruction

⚄ Cold-blooded score-settling

⚅ Misdirected passion

2 TRAGEDY

⚀ Death, out of the blue

⚁ Somebody's life is changed forever, in a bad way

⚂ Pain, followed by confusion

⚃ Death, right on time

⚄ Confusion, followed by pain

⚅ Death, after an unpleasant struggle

3 INNOCENCE

⚀ Somebody is not so innocent after all

⚁ A neighbor wanders into the situation

⚂ The wrong guy gets busted

⚃ Collateral damage

⚄ Love rears its ugly head

⚅ A well-meaning stranger intervenes

TABLES

4 GUILT

- ⚀ A visit from the (perhaps unofficial) authorities
- ⚁ Betrayed by friends
- ⚂ Somebody develops a conscience
- ⚃ Greed leads to killing
- ⚄ Someone panics
- ⚅ A showdown

5 PARANOIA

- ⚀ A stranger arrives to settle a score
- ⚁ What seems like dumb luck isn't - things are afoot
- ⚂ Two people cross paths and everything changes
- ⚃ A sudden reversal (of status, of fortune, of sympathy)
- ⚄ The thing you stole has been stolen
- ⚅ Somebody is watching, waiting for their moment

6 FAILURE

- ⚀ A stupid plan, executed to perfection
- ⚁ Something precious is on fire
- ⚂ A tiny mistake leads to ruin
- ⚃ A good plan comes unraveled
- ⚄ You thought it was taken care of but it wasn't
- ⚅ Fear leads to a fateful decision

AFTERMATH: BLACK HIGH

Zero: The worst thing in the universe. This probably doesn't include death, since death would be way better than whatever this is. Be creative and don't settle for the first "worst" thing that comes to mind – there's something darker, more awful, more wretched in there somewhere.

Black One: Horrible. You are probably dead. Other people, probably innocent people, are as well. There is no justice, there is no mercy, everything is utterly, painfully screwed and it is all – all of it – your fault.

Black Two: Brutal. Wounds that will never heal, for starters; stuff sawed off, blown off, or burned off on your way to grand, ignominious failure. Kiss whatever you care about goodbye. You may die, but you may not.

Black Three: Harsh. Shit-in-a-bag harsh, a-lifetime-of-medication harsh. A big black cloud of hurt is going to rain all over you. The things you need to happen are not going to, simple as that.

Black Four: Savage. Savage as in "something is broken or mashed." Maybe you've got a permanent limp and a bad reputation. Plus, you totally fail.

Black Five: Rough. You are getting whipped like a rented mule, for starters, and you will remember this episode for all your diminished days. The lesson you learn will be profound, lingering, and painful.

Black 6-7: Pathetic. You'll suffer, oh dear God will you suffer, and everyone will know of your malfeasance, your stupidity, your lack of common sense and decency. You're probably going to be locked up, too.

Black 8-9: Nothing to write home about. Back to where you started. Maybe sore and broke, just like yesterday and tomorrow. You probably learned something though, like how to do it right next time. Next time...

Black 10-12: Pretty good. All things considered, you're coming out of this smelling like a rose. You're a little better off - maybe you got the girl, or maybe you just didn't get caught.

Black 13+: Awesome. Insanely great. You will emerge not only unscathed, but if there's a girl involved, she's dropping her drawers. You might even get rich off this caper, who knows? Time for a new ride.

AFTERMATH: WHITE HIGH

Zero: The worst thing in the universe. This probably doesn't include death, since death would be way better than whatever this is. Be creative and don't settle for the first "worst" thing that comes to mind – there's something darker, more awful, more wretched in there somewhere.

White One: Dreadful. You are certainly dead, probably from a self-inflicted wound. People you care about are also probably dead, maybe through your own stupid, ugly failure. To say that you fucked up is an insult to fucked-upedness. You have redefined the term.

White Two: Merciless. You might not be dead on the outside but you sure as hell are dead on the inside. The emotional or mental wounds you have suffered will never heal. The future is a brick wall.

White Three: Grim. The stress and trauma from your little adventure are going to haunt you forever - bits of your soul are destroyed and you are missing a piece or two. In a few years children are going to cry when you get too close. All your plans have ended in complete ruin.

White Four: Bitter. You know what it's like to be utterly crushed, casually brought low, forced to eat your own words and stand mute and powerless before your enemies. They gloat, and you are helpless.

White Five: Miserable. You are humiliated in a big, public way, and whatever reputation you once had is now in dirty pieces all around you. You'll never think of these days without a shudder of horror at your own aggressive stupidity.

White 6-7: Weak. Hey, you're busted, beat, and broke down, but at least you've learned a lesson about human greed and frailty, right? It'll serve you well in prison, which is where you are probably headed.

White 8-9: Nothing to crow about. Not better, but not way worse, either. Maybe the car is wrecked, or your wife is leaving you, or there's a court date. But compared to some of the other people you know...

White 10-12: Not too shabby. You've made it out with dignity intact, through some fluke. There might even be a little profit, or self respect, or something. Time to throw a little party for all your friends.

White 13+: Fan-fucking-tastic. It's fat times ahead, safe and secure. That thing that would make your life better? Oh, you got it, absolutely, and then some. And then some more. Enjoy it!

TABLES

PLAYSETS

We released ourselves on our own recognizance.

Gale Snopes, *Raising Arizona*

ABOUT PLAYSETS

A Playset provides a framework you'll build on to create characters and situation. A complete Playset consists of four 36-item lists (six sub-lists of six items each), and some might have a custom Tilt list as well. The Playset you choose will inform your game in a huge way, so pick one you like or make your own. The ones included in *Fiasco* have been heavily playtested and are really solid, and more are available at the Bully Pulpit Games Website. If you are in a hurry, "Insta-Setups" have been provided that will allow you to blaze through the Setup.

MAKING PLAYSETS

Use the playsets provided if you like them, but by all means create – and share – your own. The feel of your game is tied to the content of the lists, so by changing them, you change the game. Localize. Change the time period. Alter the relationships implicit in the Relationships. Go crazy. The Relationships and Needs are likely to need very little tweaking, but Location and Object lists really define your setting, so they should get more attention. Each item should cry out for inclusion, either because it is totally crazy or deliciously prosaic.

You'll need to come up with a ton of new Elements (don't forget to mess with The Tilt if necessary). One great way to handle this is to write each six-item list's title on an individual index card, and then rotate the cards around. Everyone adds one new item to each list and rotates again. Once a card has six items, number them and set that card aside. Don't be shy about re-using big chunks of existing Playsets as well – Relationships don't change much, so consider grabbing and tweaking an existing set.

If you are feeling adventurous, think about replacing entire Details – what happens when you take away locations and replace them with burdens?

Budget a little extra time if you are building your own Playset, maybe an hour, and please share it with the world!

RELATIONSHIPS...

1 FAMILY

⚀ Parent-In-law / son or daughter-in-law

⚁ Cousins, or aunt/uncle and niece/nephew

⚂ Siblings

⚃ Parent / child or stepchild

⚄ Grandparent / grandchild

⚅ Distant / unusual / unofficial relatives

2 WORK

⚀ Former co-workers

⚁ Current co-workers

⚂ Supervisor / employee

⚃ Tradesman (mechanic, plumber, decorator, landscaper) & client

⚄ Salesman / customer

⚅ Professional (pastor, doctor, lawyer, dentist, drug dealer) & client

3 FRIENDSHIP

⚀ Manipulator / victim

⚁ Old buddies

⚂ Drug friends

⚃ Friendly rivals

⚄ Friends with benefits

⚅ Bitter social adversaries (church friends)

4 ROMANCE

⚀ Former spouses

⚁ Current spouses

⚂ Life-long crush / object of crush

⚃ One-time fling

⚄ Lovers

⚅ Former lovers

5 CRIME

⚀ Corrupt official / local big shot

⚁ Gambler / bookie

⚂ Thieves (shoplifters, burglars, car thieves)

⚃ Con man / mark

⚄ Hoodlums (racketeers, knuckleheads, delinquents)

⚅ Drug people (dealers, manufacturers, distributors)

6 COMMUNITY

⚀ Elected officials (Aldermen, mayor, commissioner)

⚁ Civic volunteers (election officials, chamber, clubs)

⚂ Church volunteers (deacons, Sunday school teacher)

⚃ Rec league, minor league, pick-up team sports

⚄ Case worker, parole officer, guardian ad litem / client

⚅ AA/Narcanon sponsor / participant

...IN A NICE SOUTHERN TOWN

NEEDS...

1 TO GET OUT

⚀ ...of this town, before they realize you took it

⚁ ...of this town, to escape family

⚂ ...of the gang

⚃ ...of a relationship with a lover

⚄ ...of the obligation to a frail relative in your care

⚅ ...of a crushing debt coming due

2 TO GET EVEN

⚀ ...with the bad people, who think they are so tough

⚁ ...with this town, for what it has turned you into

⚂ ...with a police officer

⚃ ...with a family member

⚄ ...with a co-worker

⚅ ...with a rival

3 TO GET RICH

⚀ ...through stealing a drug stash

⚁ ...through robbing a business

⚂ ...through tricking a handicapped guy

⚃ ...through the death of an elderly person

⚄ ...through political back-scratching

⚅ ...through a misplaced suitcase full of cash

PLAYSETS

4 TO GET RESPECT

⚀ ...from this town, by bringing down the machine

⚁ ...from this town, by proving your convictions

⚂ ...from your lover, by taking the fall

⚃ ...from the police, by turning in your own kin

⚄ ...from a family member, by rescuing them from ruin

⚅ ...from yourself, by finally doing it once and for all

5 TO GET THE TRUTH

⚀ ...about why they are all so shut-mouthed

⚁ ...about the Sheriff's political corruption

⚂ ...about why he really came here

⚃ ...about what she did behind The Patio

⚄ ...about your real parents

⚅ ...about the mistake that haunts you

6 TO GET LAID

⚀ ...to get it over with

⚁ ...by that sweet thing you've been thinking on

⚂ ...because you need the raise that badly

⚃ ...by an old lover, to start over

⚄ ...by an old lover, to further your scheme

⚅ ...by your sweetheart, who is acting squirrelly

...IN A NICE SOUTHERN TOWN

LOCATIONS...

1 MAIN STREET

⚀ Peace Haven Church

⚁ El Perro Alto Mexican Restaurant

⚂ Royall's Drug Store: Pharmacy in the back, soda fountain up front

⚃ Shafter and Hazelbrook, LLC, the only lawyers in town

⚄ Commercial Bank, the only bank in town

⚅ Vantage Services, medical claims processor

2 COMMERCE STREET

⚀ Suds and Duds, coin operated laundromat

⚁ Municipal building, police station, courts and City Hall

⚂ Family Medical Clinic, the only doctor in town

⚃ New Outlook, tanning salon and weight loss center

⚄ The Patio, a movie picture house

⚅ Bill Rivers' Pool Room, for pool and illegal gambling

3 OUT BY THE INTERSTATE

⚀ Chicken Hut, fast food restaurant

⚁ Davenport's Tire and Tractor, tire shop and tractor repair

⚂ Rose's Village Motel, convenient to the highway

⚃ The Quik-Pik, gas station and convenience store

⚄ Durable Paper Goods, paper bag manufacturing plant

⚅ Accurate Automotive, used cars

4 UP CENTER ROAD

⚀ J&K Gravel: Gravel, stone, and quarried materials

⚁ The old fish house, an abandoned roadhouse

⚂ Center Road Animal Care, large animal veterinarian

⚃ Lyman C. Mills Consolidated High School

⚄ Spiller's, funeral services since 1911

⚅ Charles Green Landscaping, lawn care and excavation

5 OUT AND ABOUT

⚀ Town parking lot beside the freight tracks

⚁ Red Run State Park

⚂ A farmer's field out past Surry Avenue

⚃ The ball field

⚄ Woods up around Hickory Terrace

⚅ Construction site next to Accurate Automotive

6 RESIDENCES

⚀ Van parked behind Royall's

⚁ Trailer out back of the high school

⚂ Apartment above Suds and Duds

⚃ Farmhouse up Center Road

⚄ Split-level ranch on Surry Avenue

⚅ Mansion out by Hickory Terrace

...IN A NICE SOUTHERN TOWN

PLAYSETS

OBJECTS...

1 UNTOWARD

⚀ Porn stash / sex gear

⚁ Welfare check / food stamps

⚂ Garage full of Amway products

⚃ Mink farm

⚄ Klan outfit / hate paraphernalia

⚅ Eviction notice

2 TRANSPORTATION

⚀ Golf cart

⚁ New pickup truck

⚂ Panel truck

⚃ Small plane

⚄ Pontoon party boat

⚅ Dirt bike

3 WEAPON

⚀ Shotgun

⚁ Machete

⚂ Poisonous snake

⚃ Handgun

⚄ Pipe bomb

⚅ Firefighter's Halligan tool

PLAYSETS

68

4 INFORMATION

- ⚀ Secret recipe
- ⚁ An overheard conversation
- ⚂ Legal records
- ⚃ Love letter
- ⚄ List written in a Christmas card
- ⚅ Photographs

5 VALUABLES

- ⚀ Drug stash
- ⚁ Mason jar full of gold coins
- ⚂ Comic book collection
- ⚃ Vintage car
- ⚄ Purebred animal
- ⚅ Suitcase full of cash

6 SENTIMENTAL

- ⚀ Newborn baby
- ⚁ War memorabilia
- ⚂ Roadside accident shrine
- ⚃ Mathematics trophy
- ⚄ Wedding ring
- ⚅ Heirloom silver tea set

...IN A NICE SOUTHERN TOWN

A NICE SOUTHERN
INSTA-SETUP

RELATIONSHIPS

For three players...

* Family: Siblings

* Romance: Former spouses

* Crime: Corrupt official / local big shot

For four players, add...

* Friendship: Drug friends

For five players, add...

* Work: Professional and client

NEEDS

For three players...

* To get even: With a rival

For four or five players, add...

* To get out: Of a crushing debt coming due

LOCATIONS

For three, four or five players...

* Main Street: El Perro Alto Mexican Restaurant

OBJECTS

For three or four players...

* Valuables: Suitcase full of cash

For five players, add...

* Weapon: Poisonous snake

PLAYSETS

RELATIONSHIPS...

1 FAMILY

⚀ Parent / son- or daughter-in-law

⚁ Cousins

⚂ Siblings

⚃ Parent / child or stepchild

⚄ Uncle/nephew or aunt/niece

⚅ Unrelated, but close as blood

2 WORK

⚀ Ranch hands

⚁ Miners

⚂ Supervisor / employee

⚃ Tradesman / customer (wheelwright, barber)

⚄ Salesman / customer (snake oil, mine gear, bibles)

⚅ Professional / client (pastor, doctor, lawyer, banker)

3 THE PAST

⚀ Criminal and detective

⚁ Grew up together back East

⚂ Reformed criminals

⚃ War adversaries

⚄ Both married to same spouse (sequential or tandem?)

⚅ Bad family blood

4 ROMANCE

⚀ Former spouses

⚁ Current spouses

⚂ Unvarnished lust

⚃ One-time fling

⚄ Mail-order bride and her groom

⚅ Former lovers

5 CRIME

⚀ Crime boss and toady

⚁ Gamblers

⚂ Thieves (yeggs, burglars, horse thieves)

⚃ Faith healer and patient

⚄ Outlaws (bad men, pistoleros, roughnecks)

⚅ Chinese opium seller / addict

6 COMMUNITY

⚀ Elected officials (mayor, judge, register of deeds, assayer)

⚁ Society (temperance league, brass band, vigilantes)

⚂ Church volunteers (lay readers, sexton and gravedigger)

⚃ Company / citizen (railroad or mine and shareholder)

⚄ Government / citizen (Indian agent, tax assessor)

⚅ Sheriff and deputy

...IN THE WILD WEST

NEEDS...

1 TO GET FREE

⚀ ...of this town, before everyone finds out about you

⚁ ...of a family obligation

⚂ ...of a business commitment

⚃ ...of a relationship with a lover

⚄ ...of your lot in life

⚅ ...of a crushing debt coming due

2 TO GET EVEN

⚀ ...with this town, and its small-minded inhabitants

⚁ ...with the local crime boss

⚂ ...with the Sheriff

⚃ ...with a family member

⚄ ...with the Chinese

⚅ ...with a rival

3 TO GET RICH

⚀ ...through robbing a stagecoach

⚁ ...through robbing a business

⚂ ...through fraud and trickery

⚃ ...through buying various officials

⚄ ...through violence

⚅ ...through a misplaced trunk full of bullion

4 TO GET RESPECT

⚀ ...from this town, by bringing down the machine

⚁ ...from this town, by showing everybody who's boss

⚂ ...from your lover, by proving yourself

⚃ ...from the sheriff, by ratting out your friends

⚄ ...from a family member, by rescuing them from ruin

⚅ ...from yourself, by finally doing it once and for all

5 TO GET AWAY

⚀ ...from the baying hounds of the law

⚁ ...with murder

⚂ ...from hard-riding vengeance

⚃ ...from an honest woman, ruined

⚄ ...with your reinvention of yourself

⚅ ...with a magnificent swindle

6 TO GET LAID

⚀ ...by anyone, anywhere, to dull the pain

⚁ ...by your ticket out of this burg

⚂ ...by an ambitious and beautiful saloon girl

⚃ ...to prove them all wrong

⚄ ...by your friend's spouse, to further your agenda

⚅ ...so you don't die a virgin

...IN THE WILD WEST

LOCATIONS...

1 RESIDENCES

⚀ A filthy buckboard wagon with a ragged awning and barrels for walls

⚁ A tidy Sears-bought house, crisply painted

⚂ A permanent room in the Belle-Union Boarding House

⚃ A gaudy mansion next to the dirt platted as a park

⚄ The opium den behind the White Star Laundry

⚅ A squalid apartment above the newspaper office

2 THE BRADFORD HOTEL

⚀ The storm cellar

⚁ The clerk's room, safe, and freight office

⚂ The brothel billiard parlor

⚃ The saloon

⚄ A bar girl's crib

⚅ The Governor's Suite

3 THE DECENT PART OF TOWN

⚀ The Commercial Bank

⚁ Sinclair's Dry Goods and Mercantile

⚂ The Territorial Sentinel newspaper office and print shop

⚃ First Church of Christ, Redeemer

⚄ The railroad depot and telegraph office

⚅ E.A. Lodge, Dentist

PLAYSETS

76

4 ACROSS THE TRACKS

⚀ The Fraternal Order of the Frontier Lodge Hall

⚁ White Star Chinese laundry

⚂ The Belle-Union Boarding House

⚃ Town jail

⚄ Eyck's Tack, Harness, and Stable

⚅ Boot Hill

5 UP IN THE HILLS

⚀ The Chinese camp

⚁ The hanging tree

⚂ The wagon road

⚃ Gold Creek shanty town

⚄ The Circle S Ranch

⚅ The secret cave

6 INDIAN COUNTRY

⚀ The burnt-out log cabin

⚁ The bandit hideout

⚂ The Hunkpatila Sioux camp

⚃ The prospector's hut

⚄ Pilot Rock

⚅ The Presbyterian mission at Broken Arrow

...IN THE WILD WEST

PLAYSETS

77

OBJECTS...

1 UNTOWARD

⚀ A three dollar "all night" brothel token

⚁ A mortician's black bag and a jug of phenolic acid

⚂ A vulcanized rubber "womb veil"

⚃ The skeleton of a Mescalero Apache

⚄ A Spiritualist's bag of magician's tricks

⚅ An abortionist's tools

2 TRANSPORTATION

⚀ A Kansas-Pacific railroad car

⚁ A four-horse mail coach

⚂ A safety bicycle

⚃ A railroad hand car

⚄ The guarded mine payroll mud coach

⚅ A St. Louis and San Francisco railroad boxcar

3 WEAPON

⚀ A blacksmith's tongs

⚁ A Sharps lever-action rifle

⚂ A matched set of Colt revolvers

⚃ A Sioux war club

⚄ A crate of old dynamite, weeping nitroglycerin

⚅ A 12-pound Mountain Howitzer

4 INFORMATION

⚀ An assay note on the minerals in Circle S Ranch soil

⚁ An overheard conversation about the Gold Creek strike

⚂ A freedman's manumission papers

⚃ A lady's diary

⚄ A faded wanted poster

⚅ A contract with the Pinkerton Detective Agency

5 VALUABLES

⚀ The deed to Sinclair's Dry Goods and Mercantile

⚁ A promissory note for two thousand dollars

⚂ A wad of Federal postage stamps wrapped in a kerchief

⚃ A cage of *Napaeozapus insignis*, Woodland jumping mice

⚄ A heavy sack of gold dust

⚅ The cashbox from the Bradford Hotel brothel

6 SENTIMENTAL

⚀ A newborn baby

⚁ A pretty locket with a lock of hair inside

⚂ A tiny oil portrait of a handsome soldier

⚃ A tear-stained love letter

⚄ An engraved silver goblet

⚅ A dying man's last words

...IN THE WILD WEST

A WILD WEST BOOMTOWN
INSTA-SETUP

RELATIONSHIPS

For three players...

* Family: Unrelated, but close as blood

* Crime: Crime boss and toady

* Romance: Mail-order bride and her groom

For four players, add...

* Community: Government / citizen

For five players, add...

* The Past: Both married to same spouse

NEEDS

For three players...

* To get free: of a relationship with a lover

For four or five players, add...

* To get away: From hard-riding vengeance

LOCATIONS

For three, four or five players...

* The Bradford Hotel: The saloon

OBJECTS

For three or four players...

* Information: An assay note on the minerals in Circle S Ranch soil

For five players, add...

* Sentimental: A newborn baby

RELATIONSHIPS...

1 FAMILY

⚀ Parent and child

⚁ Parent and step-child

⚂ Siblings

⚃ Cousins

⚄ Aunt or Uncle and child

⚅ Weird / distant relatives

2 WORK

⚀ Business rivals in a dying industry

⚁ Service worker and client (restaurant, bank, janitorial)

⚂ Professional supervisor and employee

⚃ Tradesman / homeowner (lawn care, plumbing, HVAC)

⚄ Salesman / homeowner (siding, drive resurfacing)

⚅ Professional / client (pastor, doctor, lawyer, banker)

3 THE PAST

⚀ Criminal and parole officer or detective

⚁ Fast friends back when all this was farm country

⚂ Cross-town sports rivals back in the day

⚃ Drunk driver and victim's next of kin

⚄ Mutual keepers of an ominous secret

⚅ Bad family blood from way back

PLAYSETS

4 ROMANCE

⚀ Divorced and remarried spouses

⚁ Current spouses

⚂ Separated spouses

⚃ One-time fling

⚄ Current lovers

⚅ Former lovers

5 CRIME

⚀ Drug manufacturer and dealer

⚁ Gambler and bookie

⚂ Thieves (shoplifters, burglars, car thieves)

⚃ Small-time vandals and ne'er-do-wells

⚄ Embezzler and company accountant

⚅ Organized crime figure and wannabe

6 COMMUNITY

⚀ Officials (judge, county supervisor, town attorney)

⚁ Society (Jaycees, Masons, historical society)

⚂ Church (shelter workers, Sunday school teachers)

⚃ Sports (rec league athletes, coaches, boosters)

⚄ Government (citizen and tax collector or parole officer)

⚅ Law (cop and volunteer or registered sex offender)

...IN A SUBURBAN COMMUNITY

PLAYSETS

NEEDS...

1 TO GET LOST

⚀ ...in your unsavory hobby

⚁ ...in a doomed affair

⚂ ...in the details of a new business

⚃ ...in the eyes of your one true love

⚄ ...in a harmless fantasy

⚅ ...before they figure it out and arrest you

2 TO GET EVEN

⚀ ...with all the two-faced bastards who ruined you

⚁ ...with the local drug dealer

⚂ ...with the "Community Policing Officer"

⚃ ...with a family member

⚄ ...with the dirty immigrants

⚅ ...with your old high school rival

3 TO GET RICH

⚀ ...through opening an improbable business

⚁ ...through robbing your boss

⚂ ...through tax fraud

⚃ ...through ripping off some drug people

⚄ ...through hurting somebody who needs hurting

⚅ ...through a re-written will

4 TO GET RESPECT

[1] ...from this town, by becoming famous

[2] ...from this town, by showing everybody who's boss

[3] ...from your lover, by making a serious commitment

[4] ...from your friends, by humiliating a cop

[5] ...from your family, by turning them in

[6] ...from yourself, by standing up for yourself at last

5 TO GET AWAY

[1] ...from your shameful past

[2] ...with murder

[3] ...from the people who are looking for you

[4] ...from your stupid family

[5] ...with the biggest lie this town has ever heard

[6] ...with the "crime" that is really justice served

6 TO GET LAID

[1] ...by anonymous party people, because why not?

[2] ...by your neighbor

[3] ...by your best friend

[4] ...to hurt someone (maybe yourself)

[5] ...to prove a point

[6] ...to get what you want

...IN A SUBURBAN COMMUNITY

LOCATIONS...

1 POPPLETON TERRACE

- ⚀ A house with a fenced-in yard on Breezeway Avenue
- ⚁ Poppleton Terrace Elementary School
- ⚂ The gazebo in Poppleton Park
- ⚃ A Breezeway Avenue house with tin-foiled windows
- ⚄ The cul-de-sac at the end of Avanti Way
- ⚅ The drainage canal behind the subdivision

2 THE SHOPS AT HOMEWOOD

- ⚀ PB&J Audio-Video
- ⚁ Fancy Cuts
- ⚂ Tile World
- ⚃ One Dollar, Period
- ⚄ Michelle's Tavern
- ⚅ Homewood Branch Library

3 REDBUD COURT

- ⚀ A crumbling trailer on blocks
- ⚁ Liberty Guns and Surplus
- ⚂ The Chicken Hut
- ⚃ A van without tires, surrounded by rotting newspapers
- ⚄ The Party House
- ⚅ A seedy rental duplex

PLAYSETS

4 PROMISE HILL

- ⚀ Promise Hill Country Club
- ⚁ Water-filled gravel pit behind the country club
- ⚂ A million dollar home on the fairway
- ⚃ The Ellis Tract, last undeveloped land in the county
- ⚄ The oak tree on top of Promise Hill
- ⚅ An unfinished mansion on Patriot Lane

5 HISTORIC DOWNTOWN

- ⚀ Ratnapriya Anand, M.D.
- ⚁ The Well Dressed Lady
- ⚂ Memories and More
- ⚃ The Sugar Mill Lofts
- ⚄ County Social Services office
- ⚅ The historic Poppleton House

6 APPLE VALLEY

- ⚀ County rec center, skate park and pool
- ⚁ A Thirties bungalow with a leaky roof
- ⚂ The Law Offices of Cockburn and Lilley, LLC
- ⚃ A tidy house with an unusual statue in the yard
- ⚄ A gutted bungalow being turned into apartments
- ⚅ Apple Valley Supermarket

...IN A SUBURBAN COMMUNITY

OBJECTS...

1 UNSAVORY

⚀ A broken police ankle monitor

⚁ Night vision goggles and flexi-cuffs

⚂ One hundred feral cats

⚃ A desiccated corpse in a duct-taped garbage bag

⚄ The charred ashes of $100,000

⚅ A replica of James T. Kirk's command chair

2 INFORMATION

⚀ A home-burned DVD

⚁ A living will, ripped in half, taped together

⚂ A digital voice recorder, accidentally left recording

⚃ A tattered birth certificate

⚄ A property survey from the 1940's

⚅ An address written on the back of a business card

3 VALUABLES

⚀ Three bags of undelivered mail

⚁ A pre-ban Heckler and Koch model 91 assault rifle

⚂ A briefcase containing one million dollars in Central American bearer bonds

⚃ A minivan stuffed with bales of marijuana

⚄ A piece of rare celebrity memorabilia

⚅ A pedigreed champion dog

PLAYSETS

88

4 SENTIMENTAL

⚀ Bronzed baby shoes

⚁ A massive engagement ring

⚂ A battered set of golf clubs

⚃ A signed photo of an ex-President

⚄ An American flag

⚅ An elaborate tombstone

5 TRANSPORTATION

⚀ A tricked-out street racing Mitsubishi Lancer

⚁ An ancient Pontiac Bonneville sedan

⚂ A Ducati 1098 sport motorcycle

⚃ An ice cream truck

⚄ A hearse

⚅ A new Toyota Prius

6 WEAPON

⚀ A hockey stick

⚁ A K-Frame revolver

⚂ A child's chemistry set

⚃ A .22 rifle

⚄ A 55 gallon drum of heating oil

⚅ A Klingon sword

...IN A SUBURBAN COMMUNITY

PLAYSETS

A SUBURBAN
INSTA-SETUP

RELATIONSHIPS IN THE SUBURBS

For three players...

* Family: Parent and step-child

* Romance: Separated spouses

* Crime: Drug manufacturer and dealer

For four players, add...

* Work: Tradesman / homeowner

For five players, add...

* The Past: Bad family blood from way back

NEEDS IN THE SUBURBS

For three players...

* To get rich: Through robbing your boss

For four or five players, add...

* To get laid: To get what you want

Locations in the suburbs

* For three, four or five players...

* Apple Valley: Apple Valley Supermarket

OBJECTS IN THE SUBURBS

For three or four players...

* Information: A home-burned DVD

For five players, add...

* Transportation: Tricked-out street racing Mitsubishi Lancer

PLAYSETS

90

RELATIONSHIPS...

1 WORK

⚀ Supervisor / worker

⚁ Co-workers

⚂ Specialist / supporter

⚃ Former co-workers

⚄ Clandestine collaborators

⚅ Professional rivals

2 FRIENDSHIP

⚀ Manipulator / victim

⚁ Bewildered first-timers

⚂ Drinking buddies

⚃ Bitter enemies

⚄ Fuck buddies

⚅ Dorm room bunkies

3 ROMANCE

⚀ Former spouses

⚁ Current spouses

⚂ Life-long crush / object of crush

⚃ One-time fling

⚄ Lovers

⚅ Former lovers

4 CRIME

⚀ Smugglers (artifacts, endangered species)

⚁ Gambler / bookie

⚂ Ecological extremists

⚃ Government contract fraudster / investigator

⚄ Hoodlums (sports enthusiasts, drunkards, delinquents)

⚅ Drug people (dealers, manufacturers, distributors)

5 COMMUNITY

⚀ Social adversaries

⚁ Search and rescue volunteers

⚂ Tour guides

⚃ Community event organizers

⚄ Visiting dignitary "handlers"

⚅ Isolated co-religionists

6 SOUL

⚀ Lifers on The Ice

⚁ The only survivors

⚂ The ones who found the body

⚃ Newbie / old timer

⚄ Two-of-a-kind misanthropes

⚅ Poet and muse

...IN MCMURDO STATION, ANTARCTICA

NEEDS...

1 TO GET OUT

⚀ ...of a work detail that is killing you

⚁ ...of a relationship that's turned weird

⚂ ...of responsibility for an accident

⚃ ...of intense scrutiny, so you can finish what you started

⚄ ...of Mactown, where too many people know your game

⚅ ...of The Ice, which is driving you insane

2 TO GET EVEN

⚀ ...with a scientist

⚁ ...with a contractor

⚂ ...with a pilot

⚃ ...with your rival

⚄ ...with an organization – the NSF, USAP, etc

⚅ ...with everybody on The Ice

3 TO GET OFF

⚀ ...on re-watching a DVD of what you did

⚁ ...on prescription painkillers

⚂ ...on secret trips out of Mactown

⚃ ...on sabotaging a scientific program

⚄ ...on destroying a reputation

⚅ ...on illicit sex

4 TO GET RESPECT

⚀ ...from everyone on The Ice, atoning for your mistake

⚁ ...from everyone on The Ice, showing them who's boss

⚂ ...from your lover, by proving your devotion

⚃ ...from the USAP, by ratting out the drug dealer

⚄ ...from a friend, by rescuing them from ruin

⚅ ...from yourself, by punishing your persecutors

5 TO GET THE TRUTH

⚀ ...about the accident

⚁ ...about the secret project

⚂ ...about someone's criminal history

⚃ ...about someone's infidelity

⚄ ...about who the visiting dignitary is

⚅ ...about the locked room in B-142

6 TO GET LAID

⚀ ...by anyone, anywhere, to dull the pain

⚁ ...by that girl/guy you've had your eye on

⚂ ...by a visitor, fast

⚃ ...by an old lover, rekindling an old romance

⚄ ...in exchange for something you need

⚅ ...by your sweetheart, who has been strangely distant

...IN MCMURDO STATION, ANTARCTICA

LOCATIONS...

1 THE WEDDELL SEA

⚀ Atop Iceberg B-15, larger than Luxembourg

⚁ Weddell seal research camp on the sea ice

⚂ Aboard the M/V American Tern, delivering supplies

⚃ Aboard the Khlebnikov, a Russian tourist icebreaker

⚄ The ATC hut at Williams Airfield, 16 km away

⚅ A research dive camp with a hole cut in the ice

2 MACTOWN: BUSINESS

⚀ Satellite receivers on Black Island, 40 km away

⚁ The tool shed inside the Carp Shop

⚂ Explosives storage shed, up the hill from Mactown

⚃ B-120, the food warehouse

⚄ B-142, Medical

⚅ B-143, the vehicle maintenance "Heavy Shop"

3 MACTOWN: PLEASURE

⚀ Hut Ten, visiting dignitaries quarters

⚁ Wells Fargo ATM

⚂ A dormitory room

⚃ B-107, Southern Exposure coffee house

⚄ The post office in B-140

⚅ B-155, the galley

PLAYSETS

4 MACTOWN: OUTDOORS

- ⚀ Observation Hill, above McMurdo Station
- ⚁ Scott's Hut, the Terra Nova Expedition's 1913 base
- ⚂ The retro yard, with cardboard containers of waste
- ⚃ An abandoned Jamesway tent near Hut Point
- ⚄ A metal shipping container
- ⚅ Inside the cab of a snow plow

5 MACTOWN: SCIENCE

- ⚀ Closet in the biology pod in the CSEC research building
- ⚁ "The Chalet", NSF headquarters
- ⚂ The Navy electronics shop in B-165
- ⚃ Naval Support Force, Antarctica weather office
- ⚄ Room 115, earth sciences pod, CSEC research building
- ⚅ B-195, atmospheric science building, road to Scott Base

6 ROSS ISLAND

- ⚀ Lower Erebus Hut, kitchen and recreation building
- ⚁ Lower Erebus Hut, research and storage building
- ⚂ Volcanic sensor array on the caldera rim
- ⚃ Inside Mt. Erebus, above the lava lake
- ⚄ The 35 kilometer ice road to McMurdo Station
- ⚅ World's largest Adelie penguin colony, at Cape Crozier

...IN MCMURDO STATION, ANTARCTICA

OBJECTS...

1 UNTOWARD

⚀ A 55 gallon urine barrel

⚁ A stalker's notebook

⚂ A secret shrine

⚃ The crashed helicopter on the Ross Island ice road

⚄ A dead seal

⚅ Candid photos of the Deputy Director

2 FORBIDDEN

⚀ A hidden hydroponics project

⚁ A one kilo baggie of marijuana

⚂ A list of people to murder

⚃ A tri-wall cardboard container labeled toxic

⚄ A lost component from the long-abandoned Martin PM-A3 Nuclear Power Plant

⚅ Five kilos of explosives and a detonator

3 TRANSPORTATION

⚀ A balloon-tired Delta vehicle rigged for passengers

⚁ An LC-130 cargo plane

⚂ A snowmachine

⚃ A fire truck

⚄ A Bell 212 helicopter

⚅ An ancient pair of cross-country skis

4 WEAPON

- ⚀ Butcher knife
- ⚁ Ice axe
- ⚂ Signal flare
- ⚃ Fire axe
- ⚄ Five liter jug of aviation fuel
- ⚅ Beretta 9mm pistol

5 INFORMATION

- ⚀ The name of the New Zealander at Scott Base with the pain pills
- ⚁ A USB drive, a spreadsheet, names and dates
- ⚂ A used dive computer in a locked toolbox
- ⚃ An overheard sat-phone call
- ⚄ The results of a keyboard logger
- ⚅ Loose talk in the Heavy Shop

6 SENTIMENTAL

- ⚀ A can of potted meat stolen from Scott's Hut
- ⚁ A dog-eared black and white photo
- ⚂ A symbol scratched into the bumper of a Spryte vehicle
- ⚃ A child's doll
- ⚄ A Hawaiian shirt
- ⚅ A cricket bat

...IN MCMURDO STATION, ANTARCTICA

AN ANTARCTIC
INSTA-SETUP

RELATIONSHIPS AT MCMURDO STATION

For three players...

* Work: Specialist / supporter

* Crime: Smugglers (artifacts, endangered species)

* Community: Visiting dignitary "handlers"

For four players, add...

* Soul: The only survivors

For five players, add...

* Friendship: Fuck buddies

NEEDS AT MCMURDO STATION

For three players...

* To get the truth: ...about who the visiting dignitary is

For four or five players, add...

* To get laid: By a visitor, fast

LOCATIONS AT MCMURDO STATION

For three, four or five players...

* Mactown Outdoors: Scott's Hut, the Terra Nova Expedition's 1913 base

OBJECTS AT MCMURDO STATION

For three or four players...

* Forbidden: Five kilos of explosives and a detonator

For five players, add...

* Sentimental: A can of potted meat stolen from Scott's Hut

REPLAY!

STEVE: Hi *Fiasco* replay reader, allow us to introduce ourselves before we play. I'm Steve. I brought the game over tonight and I've played a few times. I'm no *Fiasco* expert, though!

MONA: That is definitely true.

STEVE: Thanks, Mona, I appreciate the support. Other than games I'm into the usual stuff – delicious toast, Patrick Swayze's performance in Red Dawn, my son Henry and horror movies.

MONA: I'm Mona, the token girl, and I'm fairly new to role-playing. My favorite games so far, other than *Fiasco* of course, are *1001 Nights* and *Best Friends*. I have two sweet dogs and I like making things. I sew my own cosplay outfits and knit and have a blowtorch.

JOEL: I'm Joel. I've been gaming pretty much all my life. Right now I'm running an L5R campaign and playing the second season of a *Prime Time Adventures* show. I work for the government and that's about all I can say about that.

JEFF: Hi, I'm Jeff. Like Joel I've been playing games a long time, but only recently got interested in shorter-form games like *Fiasco*. I've got a regular D&D group that's been playing together for years. I like to cook, and I'm into anime as well.

MONA: That's all of us. Let's get this show on the road, shall we?

STEVE: Right. From here on out we're focusing on the game.

THE SETUP

The rules for The Setup begin on page 15.

JOEL: Steve, since you've played before, can you try to keep things on track and answer any rules questions if they crop up?

STEVE: Sure thing. I assume we're playing straight – no rules tweaks.

They agree and begin the Setup.

JEFF: We need a Playset, right? Any preferences?

MONA: Let's use "A Nice Southern Town."

JOEL: Sounds good. Why don't we set it in … let's see … Robin Hood, North Carolina.

JEFF: I like that; it already sounds off-kilter. How many dice do we need?

STEVE: Four players, four dice each, so 16. Eight black and eight white.

They gather the dice.

MONA: Can I roll them?

STEVE: Sure!

Mona rolls all sixteen dice:

JEFF: Who goes first?

STEVE: Who grew up in the smallest town? Not me.

JEFF: Not me either. Joel? Mona?

JOEL: 2,000 people?

MONA: You win. My home town is tiny, but not that tiny.

Joel looks at the Playset lists, reviewing Relationships, Locations, Objects and Needs in a small southern town. They are seated Joel, Steve, Mona, Jeff, so Joel is first and Jeff is last in rotation throughout the game.

JOEL: Hmm, there's only one five, and I definitely want a crime Relationship so I'll take that.

Joel writes "Relationship: Crime" on an index card and places it between himself and Steve – they will have a criminal relationship of some sort. He puts the die on top of the card.

STEVE: I'm next. How about a work Relationship between Jeff and Mona?

Steve writes "Relationship: Work" on a new index card, puts it between Jeff and Mona, and places a two die on it.

MONA: Work, huh? All right. I'll take a two and make us co-workers. Where and how, we don't know yet.

Mona finishes the Relationship card between her and Jeff by adding "Co-workers" and putting her die on it, beside the other two already on it.

JEFF: The Details will come, Mona. I want some community involvement in our story here. I'll take a six.

Jeff adds the information to a card and puts it between Mona and Steve, with the six die on top of it.

JEFF: Joel, your turn.

JOEL: Right, nobody added a specific to my criminal Relationship with Steve, so I'm going to grab another six and declare it a drug thing. Meth, I think.

STEVE: Sounds great. Let's be a skeezy husband and wife team!

JOEL: Absolutely. I'll be ... let's see ... Stephen Caney, and you can be my child bride.

STEVE: We'll see about that – let's not get too specific yet. My turn, and I'm going for the Relationship between Joel and Jeff. I'll take a one, family.

MONA: Nice. Let's just finish that up. How about a one: in-laws?

JEFF: I like that. Joel, what if I was the meth cooker's father-in-law?

STEVE: That'd make me his daughter!

JOEL: Awesome. Can your guy be the town doctor?

JEFF: Definitely. Dr. Benjamin Futrelle...

Jeff scans the Locations list for random, colorful inspiration. He spies "Hickory Terrace" and decides to throw that in.

...who lives in a mansion out by Hickory Terrace! This is getting good – I want a weapon to get between the doctor and his son-in-law.

Jeff takes a three and selects from the Objects list – he chooses the Weapon Category and authors an index card: "Object: Weapon". Joel, next in rotation, eyes the Object list and grabs a one from the dice pool.

JOEL: A shotgun. It's a short-barreled pump. Of course I'm paranoid, and I keep it around the house. It's a point of tension between me and my wife's dad.

Joel puts his die on the Object card attached to the Dr. Futrelle and Stephen Caney Relationship, and completes it by adding "Shotgun".

STEVE: What about Needs, people? I'm going to throw down the three there, as a Need for Joel and I. We need to get rich, obviously. So what do we have so far?

MONA: A creepy pair of shotgun-toting meth addicts, Stephen and Joy Caney, the wife is the black sheep of a high-class family.

JEFF: Her father's the town doctor, and Dr. Futrelle wants to make good with his son-in-law Stephen and maybe help him out, but he's scared of him.

MONA: OK, time to up the ante. I'm putting down the last six as a Need between my guy, as yet unknown, and Joy the meth princess. Somebody needs to get laid.

JOEL: I love it.

JEFF: Maybe your guy is a businessman. I'll use that last one to add a Location to our Relationship – right downtown on Main Street.

JOEL: I'll take another three and make that Royall's Drug Store.

Joel places the completed Location card for Royall's Drug Store next to Jeff and Mona's Relationship card.

MONA: Sweet. My guy's the pharmacist. His name is Pete Branch.

JEFF: We work together at the regional hospital twice a month, and I visit him at Royall's. It's one of those places with a lunch counter, right?

MONA: Right. And Pete was a classmate of the Caney's back in high school.

STEVE: Maybe we dated.

MONA: Oh! Steve, take that four and put it in our Relationship, making the Need "to get laid by an old lover, to start over."

STEVE: Oh hell yes.

MONA: Branch and Joy Futrelle were engaged before my guy went off to college. My straight-arrow pharmacist never got over her.

Steve takes the four and adds "by high school sweetheart" to the existing "Need to get laid" card, finishing it.

JOEL: We still need to know how Mona's guy Branch is currently connected to the meth princess, and how the Caney's are going to get rich.

MONA: I'll take a two and put it in your Need – you losers need to get rich by robbing a business. I think we all know whose business that is going to be.

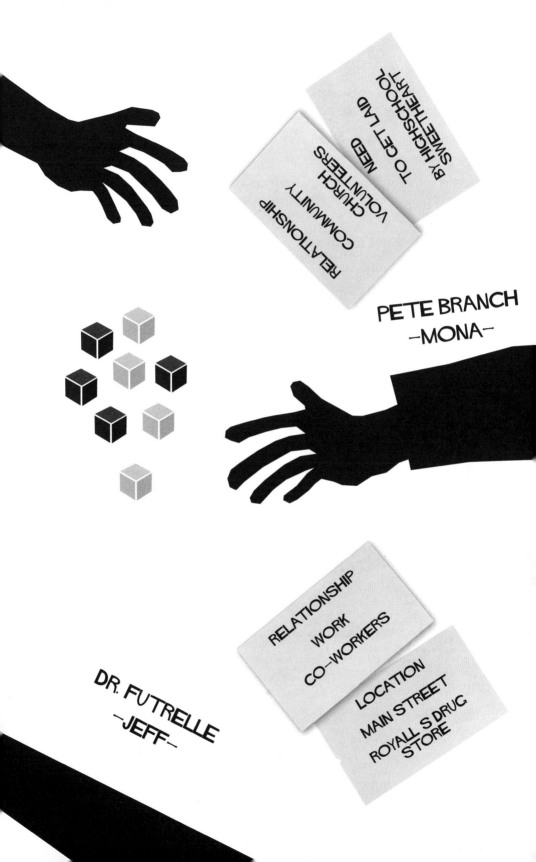

PETE BRANCH
–MONA–

DR. FUTRELLE
–JEFF–

RELATIONSHIP
TO GET LAID
BY HIGHSCHEART
SWEETHEART

NEED
CHURCH
VOLUNTEERS

RELATIONSHIP
COMMUNITY

RELATIONSHIP
WORK
CO–WORKERS

LOCATION
MAIN STREET
ROYALL S DRUG
STORE

JEFF: Cool. That leaves the last die – a two – to explain how Joy and the pharmacist are in a Relationship – it's already community, and if you want to go with it as it lays, now you guys are ... civic volunteers. Hmm.

MONA: That doesn't really fit.

STEVE: Who cares? The last die can be any number, so I think they are church volunteers. Joy may have made some bad choices, but she still has connections to the respectable community. I teach youth group! Her and Pete Branch teach youth group at Peace Haven church together.

MONA: That's horrible. I love it.

STEVE: And I'm acting really sweet to you, giving you signals, buttering you up, because we are going to fucking rob your pharmacy.

MONA: I guess that Need to get laid is sort of one-way, huh?

STEVE: Indeed, but we're both going to suffer for it. Everybody happy with this?

JEFF: It seems like poor old Dr. Futrelle is a little removed from the action.

JOEL: True, but he's got strong connections to everybody else. And there's always that shotgun. Maybe that's a fun angle – maybe he wants to get it away from Stephen Caney. I bet it won't be long before he's in the thick of things.

JEFF: Good point, Joel.

STEVE: OK, reroll all the dice into a pile and then let's play!

The Setup ends and the players begin Act One.

ACT ONE

The rules for Act One begin on page 35.

MONA: Who goes first?

STEVE: I believe Joel does. Joel?

JOEL: First scene, huh? No pressure. OK, I want to Establish.

MONA: Oh good, because we want to Resolve.

JOEL: I know you do. I want Stephen and Joy to have a scene. I want to convince her to seduce Pete Branch...

The rules for choosing to Establish a scene are on page 28.

Everyone nods – it's understood that the group will be deciding whether Stephen Caney manages to talk his wife into seducing Pete.

...It's a Friday night and we're in my trailer. "Time Cop" is on the TV, and Caney's on the couch in a bath robe, potato chip crumbs in his beard.

STEVE: Can I add something?

JOEL: Sure!

STEVE: The place smells like ammonia and chicken fat. The shotgun is propped up against an arm of the couch.

JOEL: That's a nice touch, Steve.

Steve and Joel play out the scene in character.

STEVE: We're out of everything, Stephen.

JOEL: Yeah.

STEVE: We got no food, Stephen.

JOEL: I heard you. I got some things in the works.

STEVE: Selling drugs? That's been really fruitful. You're being undercut by those Mexican guys.

JOEL: They're from El Salvador.

STEVE: Well they are moving all the meth in this town and eventually they are going to come over here and beat the shit out of you or worse.

JOEL: Maybe. I got some plans.

STEVE: What plans? What plans do you have, you nuclear genius?

JOEL: People around here don't want street-cooked mess, Joy. They want pharmaceuticals. Stuff in foil packets, so you can see where it came from, who made it.

STEVE: Terrific. So are you going to get a job with Eli Lilly? Jesus, Stephen, be sensible.

JOEL: Well, Joy, I am a sensible guy when you come right down to it. I know where all the good shit is.

STEVE: Sure, me too, Sherlock – Royall's God-damned pharmacy.

JOEL: Exactly.

STEVE: What's the matter with you? You want to rob the drug store?

JOEL: Well I do and I don't. I want to walk in with the keys and just fill up some bags after hours, no fuss and no shouting. I want you to get me the keys to the place. The code to the alarm, too. We'll do it easy.

STEVE: Me? How am I supposed to ... oh now wait a minute.

JOEL: That's right, you know the guy. You more than know him, Joy.

Steve, Mona, and Jeff all exchange glances, thinking about whether Stephen Caney is going to get what he wants.

STEVE: That was a long time ago. Me and Pete...

JOEL: You guys were the golden couple in high school I hear. Most likely to succeed and all that.

STEVE: Pete Branch is a decent guy. He teaches Sunday school, for Christ's sake.

JOEL: I bet. Look, Joy, I got it all worked out. You start teaching Sunday school up at Shady Grove with him. Make them googly eyes at him. Tell him what a bastard I am.

STEVE: That's not a stretch.

JOEL: Whatever it takes, you get him in your pocket, Joy. You get those keys.

A positive outcome for Stephen is too good to pass up. Jeff picks up a white die, and Steve and Mona nod in agreement. Jeff puts it in front of Joel and they all know how the scene will end. Steve, playing Joy, has everything he needs to know to finish the scene.

STEVE: I'm not going to seduce Pete Branch.

JOEL: Yeah you are. And you'll probably like it. Hell Joy, you can do the guy if that's what it takes. I don't care.

STEVE: That's good to know.

JOEL: You do this and I'll handle the rest. We clean the place out and it'll be money, Joy. Big money. Get out of Robin Hood money. We can move to Raleigh, Charlotte, wherever you want. It'll be the break we need. Get away from your old man.

STEVE: That sounds pretty good, Stephen.

JOEL: So you'll do it?

STEVE: Pete's so nice. It'll destroy him.

JOEL: So you'll do it?

STEVE: Yeah, I'll do it.

JOEL: And that's the scene.

MONA: That was great. You guys are terrible.

JOEL: Thanks.

Since it is Act One, Joel has to give the outcome die away. He sets his white die in front of Jeff. He's thinking that this is the start of a trend – enough white dice, and maybe he can engineer a happy ending for Dr. Futrelle in the Aftermath (see page 47), which seems satisfyingly perverse.

STEVE: I like Joy, she's so ... mean.

Steve is up next, and asks to Resolve (see page 29). Jeff, Mona and Joel set up a scene where Joy is confronted by her father, who wants her to leave Stephen. It turns into a shouting match, and Steve decides it's going to end badly for Joy. He grabs a black die and Jeff, taking the hint, browbeats her into furious silence. At the end of the scene, Steve gives the black die to Joel.

JOEL: Wow, that was rough, Steve. She really is nasty. Mona, you're up!

They begin the third scene.

MONA: You know, I want to Establish. Not sure where it's going.

STEVE: That's fine.

MONA: Pete Branch is in Royall's, nursing a cup of coffee. I'd like Dr. Futrelle to be there.

JEFF: For sure. Do you have something in mind, Mona?

MONA: Not really. Let's say Futrelle looks worried and sad.

Jeff and Mona play out the scene in character.

MONA: Hey, Doc, want some company? Mornings are slow around here.

JEFF: Sure, Pete.

MONA: How's business down at the hospital?

JEFF: Steady. The usual cuts and bruises now that school's out and the kids are back on the farm.

MONA: Yeah, it's all hay fever and corn husker's lotion here. How's the family?

JEFF: Fine, fine.

MONA: And ... Joy?

JEFF: Oh, Pete, I wish you two had stayed together. That Stephen Caney – she just married him to spite me. To punish us. He's no damn good.

MONA: Aw, he's not that bad. He loves your daughter. I've seen them around town – he really loves her, Doc.

JEFF: He's straight from the devil is what he is. He's a drug-dealing punk and if I had my way he'd be ridden out of town on a rail.

MONA: Don't talk that way.

JEFF: He keeps a loaded shotgun in his living room, Pete!

MONA: A lot of people do. Look, I know you don't like him, but you ought to try. It's been hard for me to accept it, because you know I care for Joy, but it is what it is. We don't get to change it....

There's a contemplative pause, and Mona finally breaks character.

...OK, I think this is mostly color. Not seeing a conflict. I just wanted to showcase the relationship between Pete and the Doctor.

JEFF: I really like how innocent and kind you are making Pete, Mona.

STEVE: It's excruciating.

JEFF: We've established that Pete's a wonderful guy and that I hate my son-in-law. I love it! So is it positive or negative for Pete?

JOEL: I'd say negative overall.

MONA: For sure. Defending Stephen Caney? That doesn't bode well.

They take a black die from the pool and give it to Mona. Since it is still Act One, she can't keep it and sets it in front of Joel.

JOEL: Thanks. I was hoping for nothing but white dice for my drug-dealing cretin tonight. Oh, well! Anyway, Jeff, you're up.

JEFF: Could my scene just continue the one you started?

MONA: I don't see why not. Is that legal, Steve?

STEVE: Sure! Do you want to literally keep rolling, or would you like us to change things up so you can Resolve?

JEFF: The latter, I think. Surprise me.

They begin the fourth scene, which sees all four characters interact in Royall's. Since its Dr. Futrelle in the spotlight, Joel has Stephen Caney force Joy to approach her father and apologize for their fight earlier, demonstrating the humiliating and scary hold he has over her. Jeff takes a black die, almost gets the nerve to confront Stephen Caney, and backs down. He gives the die to Joel, whose scene is next.

Two more crazy scenes are played out – some half-assed gunplay, and a comedy of errors involving Joy, the El Salvadoran gangsters and Pete Branch's Ford Escort– until it is Mona's turn again.

MONA: I don't actually have anything in mind, so I'll Resolve. Set me up, guys.

STEVE: A scene for Pete Branch.

JOEL: I've got an idea. Let's have Joy make her first move at Sunday school.

STEVE: OK by me. Are you cool with that, Mona?

MONA: Definitely, since I get to decide whether Pete falls for it or not.

STEVE: So it's a flashback to a few days before everything started getting really crazy. Shady Grove is a Baptist church, up on a hill, picture perfect. There's a little rec room for Sunday school and all morning Joy's been brushing up against him, making meaningful eye contact, that sort of thing.

JEFF: She's looking good, too – a little too good for Sunday. She smells nice.

MONA: The last kid has just been picked up. It's just the two of them, tidying up, a moment Pete's been dreading.

Mona and Steve play out the scene in character.

MONA: Glad you're here, Joy. An extra set of hands helps a lot with the Hudspeth twins.

STEVE: Oh, I know it! It was fun, though. Like old times. Remember youth group?

MONA: Oh, man, those were the days.

STEVE: We had a lot of fun, didn't we, Pete?

MONA: We sure did.

STEVE: I miss those good times.

MONA: Well, you're a married lady now, you've got certain responsibilities. You can't go running off to the swimming hole whenever you please.

STEVE: No, I sure can't. I sure can't.

MONA: Aw, Joy, you look so glum! Stephen's a nice fella. You're lucky.

STEVE: Am I?

MONA: Sure you are. I mean, look at me. What do I have to show for myself? Nothing.

STEVE: That's not true. You're still a good man, a decent man, Pete.

Steve grins.

STEVE: OK, Joy sidles up and touches his face. She looks in his eyes and gets really close.

Mona grins and picks up a black die, choosing for her character, Pete, to fail.

Pete can feel her warmth, smell her perfume – the same perfume she wore in high school.

MONA: And he turns away and grabs a broom, beet red and flustered. And she follows him, backs him into a corner.

STEVE: Pete, I'm so lonely.

MONA: And against his better judgment, against every instinct, he kisses her. Then he runs away.

JOEL: I'm so happy right now. This is all going to end in a terrible tragedy.

MONA: Oh yes.

Mona and Steve share a high-five. Mona gives Jeff the black die to go with the white die he already has in front of him.

STEVE: We're down to the final die before the Tilt, and Jeff, it's all yours.

JEFF: I want to Establish! Here's the deal, if it's OK with you, Joel.

JOEL: Bring it.

JEFF: Stephen Caney has a garbage bag full of fentanyl patches and a bullet wound in his calf. It's swollen and his shoe is full of blood and he can barely walk.

STEVE: Joy is still God knows where.

JOEL: Cool. So he's going to pay his father-in-law a visit.

JEFF: Stephen Caney wants to find out just how far he can push the old man – he wants his leg patched up, but more than that, he wants the man subordinate to him – a quavering minion, at least for the moment. He shows up at the Futrelle's upscale home late at night, filthy, bleeding, and carrying a pump shotgun.

JOEL: Fantastic. We're Resolving, too. You're so hosed, Jeff...

Joel and Jeff drop into character.

JEFF: Where is my daughter?

JOEL: I'm hurt bad.

JEFF: Where the hell is Joy?

JOEL: She's fine and I'll take you to her, but you gotta stitch up my leg first.

JEFF: What's in the bag?

JOEL: Fentanyl patches, loads of 'em.

JEFF: My God, you are the worst scum I have ever met.

JOEL: Well likewise and so forth. Now get the bullet out of my fucking leg.

JEFF: OK, Dr. Futrelle clears off the kitchen table and gets to work.

STEVE: It's a clean wound and the bullet comes out easily.

JOEL: While Futrelle is disinfecting it and putting on a bandage, Stephen Caney is ripping open a patch and slapping it on his shoulder. Then he points the shotgun at Futrelle and says, get your keys and your ATM card, old man, we're going to find Joy.

JEFF: I thought you knew where she was?

JOEL: Well, I got a good idea anyway.

JEFF: I'm not going anywhere with you, son.

Mona, Joel and Steve exchange some furtive glances and Steve reaches for a die – a black die. It's a good call, and everybody nods in agreement. Joel and Jeff look at the die and take their cue to play out a failure for Dr. Futrelle.

JOEL: Maybe you ain't and maybe you are. Maybe you'll stand up and be a man and I'll find your little girl all by myself and just take her someplace far away. Maybe without you and her Momma and all the nice people at Peace Haven church she'll fall into some kind of disrepute.

Maybe the fact that you just aided and abetted a known felon will come back to cause some kind of problem, who knows? I sure don't. And he hands the doctor the shotgun.

JEFF: Dr. Futrelle's brave front collapses, he gives in, his head hung low, and the two of them roar off into the night in his big white SUV.

Steve hands the die to Jeff, who can't keep it – he gives it back to Steve.

STEVE: Man, if you'd decided to Resolve, I totally wanted to have Stephen Caney show up at the hospital while Doc Futrelle was on duty. That'd be a different set-up entirely. That was great, though!

JEFF: Ugh, I hate your guy so much, Joel!

JOEL: Thanks, I think.

THE TILT

The rules for adding complications during the Tilt between acts are on page 39.

STEVE: Half the dice are gone. What dice do you all have? I've got one white and one black. Dang.

JOEL: Three black. Thanks for screwing up my white die dominance plan, you guys.

MONA: You asked for it. I've got a single white die.

JEFF: One black and one white.

Everybody rolls their dice. Steve rolls a six and a one, for a total of five black. Joel rolls a measly total of four black. Mona rolls her white die and gets a one. Jeff rolls a pair of sixes, one black and one white, for a grand total of zero.

JOEL: What just happened?

STEVE: You and I get to decide the Tilt, Mona.

JOEL: I rolled three black dice! How could I lose?

MONA: Sucks to be you.

STEVE: All right, we get to decide what Tilt Elements to introduce in Act Two.

The eight unused dice, rolled after The Setup, show 1, 1, 2, 3, 4, 5, 6, and 6. Their colors don't matter for calculating the Tilt.

JEFF: What's it going to be, you two?

Mona looks at the Tilt table, on page 56.

MONA: Can I go first?

STEVE: Absolutely.

MONA: I want something from Paranoia. That seems appropriate.

Mona puts forward the five.

STEVE: OK, I'll use a six for Failure. And something specific from the Paranoia list. I like "A sudden reversal", so that's a four.

MONA: Excellent...

Mona looks at the Failure sub-list.

...I'm leaning toward either "A good plan comes unraveled" or "A stupid plan, executed to perfection."

JEFF AND JOEL: Stupid plan! Stupid plan!

MONA: Tell me how you really feel, guys! OK, a stupid plan it is.

Mona takes a 1 die, and she and Steve write up two new index cards with the complications on them: "Paranoia – sudden reversal" and" failure – stupid plan".

STEVE: Cool new Elements, guys. Remember that these are community property, and we can all think about how they could be incorporated into the story. OK, we're done with Act One. Let's take a break! Who wants a root beer?

They all relax – stretch, get snacks, use the restroom and talk about the game. When everyone is ready, Act Two begins with the dice from Act One still in place – Joel has three black, Mona has one white, and both Steve and Jeff have one die of each color.

ACT TWO

The rules for Act Two are on page 43.

So far eight of the sixteen dice have been allocated. Act Two plays out in the same fashion as Act One, with scenes in rotation, and a die allocated after the conclusion of each. Unlike in Act One, players keep the outcome dice throughout Act Two.

The unfolding disaster escalates as Pete Branch tries to defend Joy from a gang of hardened narcotrafficantes and Stephen Caney and Dr. Futrelle try to enlist the help of the sleepy local sheriff. Eventually, Mona grabs the final die, declares it a failure (the final die always being wild), and Act Two ends with a bang as Stephen Caney's shotgun goes off.

MONA: Hooray! What a train wreck. In a good way.

THE AFTERMATH

The rules for the Aftermath are on page 47.

STEVE: OK, you know what time it is. What dice do we have? I'm looking at two white and two black.

JOEL: Three black and two white.

JEFF: Two and two.

MONA: Two white and one black.

STEVE: All right then – what we need to do now is roll our dice and add them up by color, subtracting one total from the other. You don't want to get zero. I'm looking at you, Jeff.

JEFF: Why don't I want zero again? Because I'm... going to get zero.

STEVE: Zero is the worst possible outcome. A high number in black or white is a good outcome. A happy ending. That's why you don't want the same number of dice in each color.

MONA: Uh oh.

They roll, adding each color and then subtracting the low total from the high total. Steve rolls a three and a two on white and a six and two on black, for a total of five white and eight black; his end result is three black. After rolling, they consult the Aftermath table on page 58.

STEVE: Three black. "Harsh" – that's about right.

JOEL: Two black. Ouch. "Brutal."

JEFF: Unbelievable. Dead even again. Holy crap, what's the worst thing in the universe to Dr. Futrelle?

JOEL: Going to jail for killing his son-in-law maybe?

MONA: Huh, look at that, two white threes and a one black – five white. Miserable and humiliated but not too bad, makes sense. So Pete's going to skate out of this mess, minus his good name. Who would have figured?

STEVE: Looks like we're hip-deep in the Aftermath. Ready for the montage?

JEFF AND MONA: Yes!

JOEL: OK, we know what to do.

Jeff takes one of his four dice.

JEFF: This is Dr. Futrelle, his eyes closed, shooting Stephen Caney in the back with the shotgun.

JOEL: That was quick.

Mona takes one of her three dice.

MONA: This is Pete emptying the till at the pharmacy into a duffel bag.

The players continue picking up dice and narrating.

STEVE: Nice! This is Joy nervously smoking a cigarette, waiting for Pete in the car.

JOEL: This is Stephen Caney writhing in a pool of his own blood, struggling to breathe and mouthing the word "why?"

JEFF: Flash-forward, This is Dr. Futrelle in a courtroom, nodding his head as a judge berates him.

MONA: This is Pete in the darkened pharmacy, calling the police.

STEVE: This is Joy in handcuffs, spread out on the hood of her car, with a detective talking with Pete.

MONA: I really need more dice.

JOEL: Have some of mine.

MONA: Is that legal?

STEVE: Go for it.

MONA: This is Pete retrieving the duffel bag from the dumpster the next day.

JOEL: Awesome.

JEFF: This is Dr. Futrelle, in prison, learning that his daughter was sentenced to five years for a drug-related robbery.

STEVE: This is Joy, in a bare knuckle brawl in the prison rec yard.

MONA: And this is Pete Branch back at his old job at Royall's, like nothing had happened. He's changed though; he's got a dark aspect about him. He's a bad man now – everybody in town knows what happened, even if the law never caught up with him. He's sort of a pariah.

STEVE: Cry me a river.

MONA: Holy cow. Yep, I think that's a wrap, guys!

JEFF: I love these people. Good game.

DESIGNER'S NOTES

I'm gonna buy a set of Lexus convertibles in every color.

Troy Barlow, Three Kings

Thanks for playing *Fiasco*. I hope you really enjoy it, and that you'll share your misbegotten capers with me – I'd love to hear from you!

Part of *Fiasco*'s design process was to think pretty hard about GM-less play, the role of authority at the table, and how to communicate procedures in a clear and effective way that leads to great play. Some of these ruminations didn't have a place in the rules, but I wanted to share them anyway.

A role-playing game is a social activity that employs a weird and volatile mix of creativity, cooperation, and competition. Some games handle this stuff by clearly dividing authority – the usual model is a bunch of people reacting to the schemes of one guy in charge of creating the situation and providing the adversity. As far as I'm concerned the guy in charge has all the fun, so in *Fiasco* the authority is evenly divided, and everyone is making stuff up and putting pressure on their friend's characters all the time. For some people this is a very friendly and natural arrangement, but for others it might seem a little crazy. Here's some advice if you find yourself in the crazy camp:

Authority means both freedom and responsibility – you're free to invent new people, places, and situations, but you have the responsibility to listen to your friends and make them look good. If there's any real competition in *Fiasco*, it is the competition to offer the most interesting, satisfying stuff for other people to work with. Usually, the most entertaining elements are the ones that cause the most trouble. If you listen carefully, you'll probably hear your friends tell you what the perfect complications will be for their characters. The choices they make as you set up the game, the sorts of scenes they choose, and their actions at the table are all flags they are waving, telling you where to apply pressure and offer them difficult choices. I can't stress enough how important it is to listen.

While you have wide-open authority to introduce plot twists and new characters, you don't need to endlessly introduce new stuff. In fact, don't! Once the general outline of the game has emerged, it's much better to

122

build on what's already been established. Return to and amplify things that have already been touched on and your game will get very intense. If you're ever unsure how to proceed, there are a couple of tricks I use all the time. The first is to review previous scenes and see if there's something fascinating that happened that could be reincorporated, maybe in new ways. The second is to glance at the Relationships and Details in play, and match up a couple that have not been used together. The third – heartily recommended and more or less in constant use when I play – is to throw up your hands and ask for suggestions. Chances are good that somebody has seen an interesting way forward that you would never have thought of.

Of course it's important to check in with your friends and make sure everybody is on board with your ideas – seek consensus and work together to craft the most engaging and exciting story you can. You'll want to be on the same page when it comes to issues like character ownership (can I say that your guy does something? Can I "make" him do something if I choose to succeed in a conflict?) and framing scenes (Can I jump in with a good idea? Can I introduce something that totally changes the plot?). Wherever you and your friends want to come down on these issues is fine, as long as you are in agreement.

One last note about this style of play – *Fiasco* (and all games without a GM, really) benefits from a facilitator. If one player has a firm grasp on the rules, let them be a procedural resource during play. They've probably got a good handle on how the game should be paced, so let them move things along or encourage folks to linger over a particularly juicy scene as appropriate. A facilitator doesn't get any extra authority, but they can be very helpful in nudging the game in the right direction. This tends to emerge naturally, but there's nothing wrong with calling it out in advance.

Thanks again!

JASON

jason@bullypulpitgames.com

FILMOGRAPHY

There are a zillion films that are inspirational for *Fiasco*. Here are 54 of my favorites.

FOUR NOTE-PERFECT FIASCOS

* Blood Simple
* Burn After Reading
* Fargo
* A Simple Plan

TEN HISTORICAL GOATSCREWS

* Bad Day at Black Rock
* A Big Hand for a Little Lady
* Drugstore Cowboy
* Guizi Lai Le (Devils on the Doorstep)
* The Bank Job
* L.A. Confidential
* Miller's Crossing
* O Brother, Where Art Thou?
* The Proposition
* True Grit

TEN LESS-LETHAL CLUSTERFUCKS

* Bad Santa
* Bottle Rocket
* A Fish Called Wanda
* Observe and Report
* Office Space
* O Homem Que Copiava (The Man Who Copied)
* Next Day Air
* Crna Macka, Beli Macor (Black Cat, White Cat)
* Raising Arizona
* Primer

TEN UGLY BLOODBATHS

* Buffalo Soldiers
* A History of Violence
* In Bruges
* Lock Stock and Two Smoking Barrels
* Pineapple Express
* Three Kings
* Shaun of the Dead
* Snatch
* The Way of the Gun
* True Romance

TEN INTERNATIONAL SHITSTORMS

* Boksuneun Naui Geot (Sympathy for Mr. Vengeance)
* Cidade de Deus (City of God)
* Coup de Torchon (Clean Slate)
* Nueve Reinas (Nine Queens)
* Bande à Part (Band of Outsiders)
* Le Poulpe (The Octopus)
* Du Rafifi Chez les Hommes (Rififi)
* Soliti ignoti, I (Big Deal on Madonna Street)
* Topkapi
* You Hua Hao Hao Shuo (Keep Cool)

TEN CRIMES THAT DO NOT PAY

* Before the Devil Knows You're Dead
* Bound
* Thelma and Louise
* Heist
* Jackie Brown
* Let's Do It Again
* Out of Sight
* Shallow Grave
* Two Days in the Valley
* Very Bad Things

CHEAT SHEET

THE SETUP, SEE PAGE 15

* Choose a Playset.

* Roll a bunch of dice into a central pile.

* Develop a web of Relationships and Details.

* Create characters attached to those Relationships and Details.

* Put all the dice back into a central pile.

PLAYING SCENES, SEE PAGE 27

* When it is your turn, your character is in the spotlight. Choose to Establish or Resolve the scene.

* If you are Establishing, create a scene. If you are Resolving, ask your friends to create a scene for your character.

* Begin the scene. At some point during the scene, determine the outcome.

* If you Established, accept a die from your friends. If you Resolved, choose a die and the outcome.

* If it is Act One, give the outcome die away to another player. If it is Act Two, keep the outcome die.

* Finish the scene, informed by the outcome die color.

ACT ONE, SEE PAGE 35

* Take turns. When it is your turn, your character gets a scene.

* When only half the dice remain in the central pile, Act One ends.

THE TILT, SEE PAGE 39

* At the end of Act One, roll the dice in front of you. Do some dice math.

* If you have the high number of either color, you will help add a pair of complications.

* Roll the unused dice in the central pile.

* Consult the Tilt table on page 56 and choose two Elements.

* Reassemble the central die pile. Keep dice already assigned in Act One.

* Take a break; stretch and get a snack. Talk about where the game is heading.

ACT TWO, SEE PAGE 43

* Take turns. When it is your turn, you get a scene.

* Tilt the hell out of it!

* The final die is wild – it can be either black or white. Once the final die has been allocated, Act Two ends.

THE AFTERMATH, SEE PAGE 47

* Roll all the dice in front of your character. Total them by color, as in the Tilt.

* Consult the Aftermath table on page 58.

* Play the Aftermath as a montage, with one "this is" statement per die associated with your character.

* When you are out of dice, your story is over.

RESOURCES

* **Bully Pulpit Games Website**

   www.bullypulpitgames.com

* **Bully Pulpit Games Youtube Channel**

   www.youtube.com/user/bullypulpitgames

* **Bully Pulpit Games Business Contact**

   steve@bullypulpitgames.com

* **Bully Pulpit Games Nerd Contact**

   jason@bullypulpitgames.com

* **General Game Chatter**

   www.story-games.com/forums/

* **News of the Weird**

   newsoftheweird.blogspot.com/

* **The Smoking Gun**

   www.thesmokinggun.com/

* **Disposing of Corpses**

   ask.metafilter.com/7921/

* **Making A Fake ID**

   www.wikihow.com/Make-a-Fake-ID

* **Avoiding a Bear Mauling**

   dnr.alaska.gov/parks/safety/bears.htm

* **Cousin Marriage by State**

   www.cousincouples.com/?page=states

* **Distilling Alcohol from Hand Sanitizer**

   www.instructables.com/answers/
   Is-it-possible-to-extract-alcohol-from-hand-saniti/

INDEX

Act One 31, 35–38

    Act One (Replay) 108

Act Two 31, 43–46

    Act Two (Replay) 119

Aftermath 12, 47–50

    Tables 58

Blowtorch (tool) 101

Category 12

Characters 19

    Creating (Replay) 104–105

    Death of 34

Cheat Sheet 126–127

Color Scenes 34

Details 12, 17–18, 21

Dice 12

    Why Die Choice Matters 33

Element 13

Establish 13, 28, 30

    Establishing (Replay) 109

Facilitation (role) 123

Fentanyl patches 116

Filmography 124–125

Getting to the Good Stuff 9

Glossary 12

Hang gliding 8

Language, bad fucking 11

Locations, Needs and Objects 18, 23–25. *See also* Details

Overview 10

Playsets (Definition, Choosing, Creating) 13, 16, 60

      Playset: Boomtown 71–80

      Playset: Main Street 61–70

      Playset: Tales From Suburbia 81–90

      Playset: The Ice 91–100

Relationships 13, 17–19, 21

Replay 101–121

Resolve 13, 29, 30

      Resolving (Replay) 113

Resources 128

Scenes 27–34, 36, 44

Setup 10, 13, 15–26

      Setup (Replay) 102

SUV, big white 117

Table of Contents 7

Taking a break 41

Things to Look For

      Act One 37

      Act Two 45

      Aftermath 50

      Scenes 32

      Setup 20

      Tilt 42

Tilt 13, 39–42, 44

      Table 56

      Tilt (Replay) 117

THE FIASCO COMPANION

The Fiasco Companion is a supplement for *Fiasco*, the award-winning game of small time capers gone wrong. The book includes in-depth discussion of common pitfalls and solid techniques for making *Fiasco* games excellent, as well as advice for writing your own Playsets and hacking the rules. In addition, the *Companion* features exciting rules variants, new Tilt and Aftermath tables and four new Playsets. The book also features a foreword by Wil Wheaton and interviews with an enthusiastic and growing cohort who are taking *Fiasco* into the classroom, the writer's room, and up on stage.

ANOTHER SQUARE DEAL FROM YOUR FRIENDS AT

Visit us at *www.bullypulpitgames.com*
for an astonishing array of free stuff!